Stock Market
Forecasting for
Alert Investors

Stock Market Forecasting for Alert Investors

John C. Touhey

A Division of
American Management Associations

For Kris

Library of Congress Cataloging in Publication Data

Touhey, John C
  Stock market forecasting for alert investors.

  Includes index.
  1. Stock price forecasting. 2. Investments.
I. Title.
HG4636.T68   332.63′222   80-12878
ISBN 0-8144-5610-3

First Printing

Preface

THIS book has been written for the individual who wants to take responsibility for managing his own investments. Most books on the stock market offer very little to the person who is willing to devote some time and thought to the realization of superior investment returns. The briefest examination of recent best-sellers on the stock market indicates two dominant approaches, and neither is of much value to the alert investor. On one side, the prospective investor is beset with such nonsense as *How to Make Millions from Friday's Financial Fiasco.* To the other side lie the sober and respectable tomes which advise us to buy the telephone company.

Stock Market Forecasting for Alert Investors is written for the prospective investor who is properly skeptical of the hasty and heedless profits promised by the get-rich-quick books but who also aspires to something more rewarding than a 5 percent annual dividend in times of 18 percent inflation. Its approach to market investment is based on two interrelated assumptions. It is a fact that the major bull and bear markets of the last two decades have consistently been signaled by changes in several economic indicators. Our first assumption is simply that those indicators which have most accurately forecast previous market cycles will predict future market cycles more accurately than any other forecasting methods.

Because future market cycles will not mirror previous market cycles in every respect, I estimate the accuracy of the method presented in Chapter 1 at 80 percent to 85 percent. In support of this claim, Chapter 2 reports the results of this forecasting method on a month-by-month basis for 13 years, one of the longest and most detailed market forecasting demonstrations to be published anywhere.

The second assumption of this book is that individuals who take responsibility for their own investments will obtain better returns than those who entrust their money to stockbrokers, mutual fund operators, trust officers, and most other professional money managers. With the possible exception of a few extraordinarily competent investment advisers (whose fees are beyond the reach of all but the richest investor), the record of professional money management on Wall Street has been dismal, and the speculative excesses of the 1960s and 1970s have driven many individuals from stocks to equally ill-advised speculations in real estate, metals, commodities, and gems. Yet, while Wall Street's reputation has fallen through the late 1970s, it is ironic that selected common stocks now appear to offer greater bargains for alert investors than at any time since the 1950s.

But understanding that the market professionals are no more capable and knowledgeable than the individual investor is only the first step toward removing the mystery and hocus pocus from stock price forecasting. The next step is to learn to forecast stock prices for oneself, and this book is intended to show how this is done. The final step to superior investment returns lies in the diligent and consistent application of the eleven market indicators and six stock selectors described in Chapters 1 and 3. Here, as in nearly all else, the reader who applies himself most intelligently and determinedly to the task at hand may expect the greatest success.

John C. Touhey

Contents

1/Market Forecasting: Eleven Predictors

IF you want to make money from buying and selling stocks, you have to know where the market is going. Knowledge of future market averages is far more important to winning the market game than attempting to predict future prices of individual stocks without market forecasting. The belief that an especially strong stock will advance against major market declines has cost investors billions of dollars, and the misconception that weak stocks can't advance in rising markets has cost billions of dollars in missed opportunities. But neither mistake will happen to you if you recognize that overall market forecasting is more important than individual stock selection. Here's some evidence that demonstrates the importance of this principle.

For Table 1, I simply took the first 100 common stocks listed in *Moody's Handbook of Common Stocks*. All trade on the New York Stock Exchange. The first column of Table 1 shows the selling price of each stock at the top (January 1973) of the 1971–72 bull market. The second column shows the prices of the same stocks at the bottom (October 1974) of the 1973–74 bear market, and the last column shows the prices in January 1977, the same month our last bull market topped out.

Look carefully at Table 1, because the story in these prices means the difference between winning and losing the stock market game. First, you should note that 97 of the 100 issues declined in the 1973–1974 bear market. Now take a look at the three exceptions. American Stores advanced a single

TABLE 1

Stock prices at end of bull and bear markets.

	January 1973	October 1974	January 1977
Abbott Laboratories	40	15	49
ACF Industries	48	29	52
Acme-Cleveland	17	7	13
Addressograph-Multigraph	34	3	10
Aetna Life & Casualty	80	30	71
Airco	18	10	30
Air Products and Chemicals	75	68	128
Akzona	31	8	18
Alberto-Culver	29	4	8
Alco Standard	10	6	19
Alexander's	9	2	7
Allegheny Ludlum Industries	33	20	37
Allegheny Power System	24	11	22
Allied Chemical	49	23	36
Allied Products	22	11	15
Allied Stores	39	15	46
Allis-Chalmers	12	6	22
Alpha Portland Industries	17	6	16
Alcoa	39	28	53
Amax	33	31	59
Ambac Industries	14	5	23
Amerace	26	11	17
Amerada Hess	48	12	31
American Air Filter	40	5	18
American Airlines	25	4	15
American Bakeries	11	3	12
American Brands	45	27	46
American Broadcasting	80	22	79
American Building Maintenance	47	4	10
American Can	31	22	39
American Cyanamid	32	17	28
American District Telegraph	61	15	26
American Electric Power	30	13	25
American General Insurance	21	7	21
American Hoist & Derrick	17	7	18
American Home Products	124	78	89
American Hospital Supply	52	18	28
American Motors	8	3	4
American Natural Gas	47	26	44
American Standard	12	7	30
American Sterilizer	40	11	12
American Stores	22	23	48

	January 1973	October 1974	January 1977
American Telephone & Telegraph	55	39	65
Ametek	18	9	29
AMF	57	9	20
Amfac	31	12	14
AMP	126	61	84
Amstar	30	23	44
Amsted Industries	44	32	108
Anaconda	29	16	24
Anchor Hocking	29	12	27
Anderson, Clayton	55	31	101
ARA Services	155	47	78
Archer-Daniels-Midland	24	26	49
Arizona Public Service	24	11	19
Arkansas Louisiana Gas	27	15	37
Armco Steel	26	18	31
Armstrong Cork	34	14	25
Armstrong Rubber	38	11	24
Arvin Industries	26	4	17
Asarco	21	14	16
Ashland Oil	33	15	34
Associated Dry Goods	54	13	33
Atlanta Gas & Light	15	8	15
Atlantic City Electric	23	12	24
Atlantic Richfield	113	73	118
Automatic Data Processing	94	20	58
Avery International	43	22	19
Avnet	12	4	17
Avon Products	138	18	38
Babcock & Wilcox	26	11	36
Bache Group	10	2	8
Baker International	71	45	92
Baltimore Gas & Electric	31	12	28
Ban Cal Tri-State	26	10	16
Bankers Trust New York	68	29	38
Bank of New York	39	9	37
Barnes Group	33	16	39
Bausch & Lomb	24	22	25
Baxter Laboratories	61	24	35
Bearings	59	21	62
Beatrice Foods	30	13	28
Beckman Instruments	45	17	56
Becton, Dickinson	44	21	32
Beech Aircraft	24	10	35
Belco Petroleum	16	9	25
Belden	30	12	25

TABLE 1 (*Continued*)

	January 1973	October 1974	January 1977
Belding Heminway	13	4	8
Bell & Howell	56	8	19
Bemis	26	11	23
Bendix	51	20	56
Beneficial	53	11	27
Berkey Photo	22	1	4
Bethlehem Steel	28	23	37
Big Three Industries	50	33	99
Black & Decker	117	61	56
Bliss & Laughlin Industries	21	11	28
Blue Bell	38	12	59
Boeing	26	11	43
Boise Cascade	10	10	33

point (from 22 to 23), Archer-Daniels-Midland was up two points (from 24 to 26), and Boise Cascade was unchanged at 10. Not only is it extremely difficult to buy the individual stocks which will advance in major bear markets, but it is impossible to make much money even if you're lucky enough to find the exceptions.

The second and third columns of Table 1 tell the opposite story for bull markets. Virtually all stocks rise. Of the 100 issues shown in Table 1, 98 advanced in the bull market from October 1974 to January 1977. Moreover, the two losing stocks, Avery International and Black & Decker, showed only minor declines.

The entire point of this demonstration is to convince you that you must forecast the market averages in order to win the game. Forecasting the prices of individual stocks is also important, but it should always take second place to forecasting the overall market. In summary, most stocks eventually move with the major market swings, and the exceptions aren't worth bothering about.

There are some market professionals (who should know better) and many amateurs who argue that the largest and strongest companies are the best purchases in bear markets.

This is wrong. There are no good stock purchases in bear markets! The 30 companies which comprise the Dow-Jones industrial average are among the largest and best-financed corporations in the world. Some of these companies appear in Table 1: Allied Chemical, Alcoa, American Can, AT&T, and Bethlehem Steel. In Table 2 you can see the same price information for the 24 remaining companies. Note that every stock except United States Steel declined in the bear market and that all 24 issues advanced in the bull market.

What you have seen applies to all major stock market cycles, and it also applies to the thousands of other issues listed on the two New York and several regional stock exchanges.

TABLE 2
Prices of 24 Dow-Jones stocks at the end of bull and bear markets.

	January 1973	October 1974	January 1977
Chrysler	44	7	20
Du Pont	186	84	135
Eastman Kodak	151	57	82
Esmark	39	21	43
Exxon	92	54	108
General Electric	75	30	52
General Foods	30	16	32
General Motors	84	28	79
Goodyear	31	11	23
Inland Container	38	19	34
International Harvester	39	16	32
International Paper	40	31	63
Johns-Manville	33	14	37
Minnesota Mining & Manufacturing	87	44	57
Owens-Illinois	40	29	54
Procter & Gamble	120	67	93
Sears, Roebuck	123	41	63
Standard Oil of California	89	41	81
Texaco	43	20	27
Union Carbide	51	31	60
United Technologies	46	22	74
U.S. Steel	31	36	71
Westinghouse Electric	47	8	17
Woolworth	31	8	24

So the next time your broker, banker, father-in-law, or neighbor says he has a hot stock which will go up "even if the market drops," you should know that it's a very unlikely possibility.

FORECASTING MARKET AVERAGES

I hope you are now convinced that trying to predict individual stock prices without forecasting the market is putting the cart before the horse. If you still think you can buy the occasional winner in a bear market and sell the occasional loser in a bull market, you are searching for a needle in a haystack. You might succeed, of course, but more probably you will lose money. This is why you must learn to forecast the market averages first. Only then does it pay to consider which stocks to buy and sell for each type of forecast.

How does one forecast the market averages? Since it will help you to know a little about the history of what we are forecasting, let's take a look at the last 50 years of the Dow-Jones industrial average. Figure 1 begins with the great crash of 1929. After the Dow reached 380 in the late summer of 1929, the average dropped to 200 by the end of that year. It rebounded to 300 in 1930, but the next two years were downhill: the average fell below 40 at the bottom of the Great Depression. A five-year bull market then carried the Dow back to 180 in August 1937, and the next bear swing bottomed out at 100 in 1938. The market did nothing until Pearl Harbor, but it climbed back to 200 by the end of World War II. Except for brief declines in 1946 and 1953, the market advanced in every post-war year until it reached 500 in mid-1957. A sharp but short bear swing then clipped 80 points from the average, but in 1958 and 1959 the Dow picked up another 250 points to finish just below 700. The decades of the 1960s and 1970s have seen the wildest and most frequent swings, and those are the most important

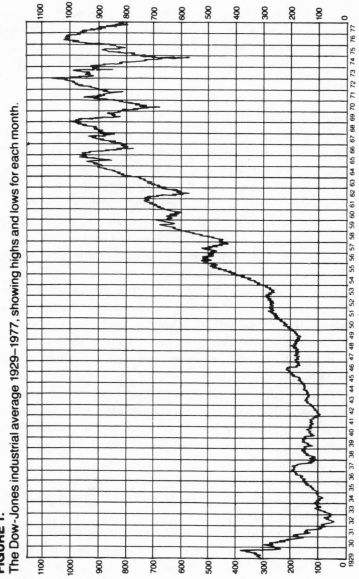

FIGURE 1.
The Dow-Jones industrial average 1929–1977, showing highs and lows for each month.

years for us. There were important bull markets in 1961, 1963, 1964, 1965, 1967, 1968, 1971, 1972, 1975, and 1976, and there were major bear markets in 1960, 1962, 1966, 1969, 1973, 1974, and 1977. 1970 was the only year in which the market finished close to where it began, and this resulted from a 300-point round trip from 800 to 650 and back again.

The lesson of this short history is clear: the market is nearly always moving. By this time next year the market will probably have moved quite a bit higher or lower. How much higher or lower? The exact percentage varies from year to year, but it is usually enough to earn you a handsome profit if you forecast the next 12 months correctly, and a whopping tax deduction if you guess wrong. Except for six years a long way back (1939, 1940, 1941, 1947, 1948, and 1949) the stock market simply hasn't stood still. The purpose of this book is to show you how to forecast these year-to-year changes in stock market prices.

Can the market averages be forecast correctly? The answer is yes, about 80 percent to 85 percent of the time. Is market forecasting difficult? Not especially, but it does take some work. You're also going to need some important background information before we get started. So here's your background.

The economy of the United States alternates between booms and busts. Professional economists prefer to speak of business "expansions" and "contractions," which follow each other in cycles. In the last 120 years or so, the U.S. economy has been through about 25 complete cycles. In order to predict and control the business cycle, economists gather and study large quantities of information, most of which have no connection to stock prices.

Here's how the stock market fits into this picture of the nation's business cycle. Major swings in the stock market run several months ahead of each period of expansion and each period of contraction. In other words, when a bear market begins, total industrial production peaks several months later. When a bull market gets under way, the economy turns up a few months later.

By how many months does the stock market run ahead of the general economy? There is no final answer, but the lead time is usually between five and ten months. Since the stock market is probably the most reliable single forecaster of the business cycle, this explains why so many traders are caught unaware when the market turns. Business conditions still look good when a bear market gets under way, and they look terrible just before the next bull market begins.

HOW TO FORECAST THE FORECASTER

While it's important to know that the market averages are forecasters of business cycles, our problem is to forecast the forecaster. Fortunately, there are several other indicators which also forecast the business cycle. Although all these leading indicators run ahead of the business cycle, the great majority of indicators lag far behind the market, so they are of no use in forecasting stock prices. But there are at least 11 leading indicators which run so far ahead of the business cycle that they frequently run ahead of the market averages as well. These indicators are the most reliable and consistent predictors of the market averages. Here they are:

PREDICTOR 1: 90-Day Treasury Bill Yield
When 90-day treasury bills yield less than 6 percent interest, the market will advance. When treasury bills yield more than 6 percent, the market will decline.

PREDICTOR 2: Total Time Savings Deposits
When the total of time savings deposits increases, the market will advance. When the total of time savings deposits decreases, the market will decline.

PREDICTOR 3: Authorized Housing Permits
When the number of authorized housing permits

increases, the market will advance. When the number of housing permits decreases, the market will decline.

PREDICTOR 4: Brokers' Cash Accounts
When the amount of brokers' cash accounts increases, the market will advance. When the amount of brokers' cash accounts decreases, the market will decline.

PREDICTOR 5: Stock Exchange Call Loan Interest Rate
When interest rates on call loans decrease, the market will advance. When rates on call loans increase, the market will decline.

PREDICTOR 6: Real Earnings
When real earnings (wages divided by inflation) of industrial workers increase, the market will advance. When real earnings of industrial workers decrease, the market will decline.

PREDICTOR 7: Bankers' Security Loans
When the amount of bankers' security loans increases, the market will advance. When the amount of bankers' security loans decreases, the market will decline.

PREDICTOR 8: Brokers' Total Margin Credit
When brokers' total margin credit increases, the market will advance. When brokers' total margin credit decreases, the market will decline.

PREDICTOR 9: Gold Prices
When the price of gold decreases, the market will advance. When the price of gold increases, the market will decline.

PREDICTOR 10: Bond Yield/Prime Rate Ratio
When the cost of short-term corporate borrowing is less than the yield from long-term bonds, the market will advance. When the cost of short-term corporate borrowing exceeds the yield from bonds, the market will decline.

PREDICTOR 11: U.S. Federal Deficit
When the federal deficit increases, the market will advance. When the federal deficit decreases or there is a surplus, the market will decline.

If these 11 predictors look pretty complicated at this point, each will become more familiar as we work through the list. For each predictor, you will be given the following information:

1. Why does it work?
2. How well does it forecast?
3. How is it used?
4. How well has it worked in the past?
5. How well will it work in the future?
6. Where do I find it?

But before we get started, I want you to study Figure 2, which shows the last 13 years (1965–1977) of *Standard & Poor's* average of 500 common stocks. The S&P 500 isn't as well known as the Dow-Jones industrial average, but it is a somewhat better measure of the general market since it consists of 470 more stocks. Here's a quick summary of the last 13 years of stock prices, using the S&P 500 as the market average. 1965 was the last year of a bull market in which the average rose from 86 to 93 before it topped out the following January. 1966 wasn't a full-fledged bear market, but the average dropped from 93 to 78 between January and October. From late 1966 through 1967 the average rose from 78 to 96, and after a shaky start in early 1968, it advanced to 107 by December. 1969–1970 encompassed an 18-month bear market that carried the average down to 77 from a high of 107, a loss of 28 percent. Through the second half of 1970 and all of 1971 the next bull swing carried the market back to 100, and the greatest bull market of all topped out in January 1973 at 118. The two-year bear market of 1973–1974 recorded the worst decline since the crashes of 1929 and 1937, a total loss of 42 percent. The first swing of the 1975–1976 bull market returned the average from 67 to 90, a 35 percent increase; and the market reached 107 at the end of 1976, a 20 percent advance. Finally, the 1977 market

FIGURE 2.
Standard & Poor's average of 500 stocks 1965–1977.

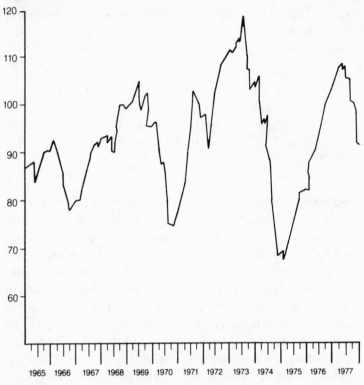

declined from 107 to 91, a 15 percent decline in the last year under study.

A MEDIOCRE STRATEGY

If you had purchased stocks at the beginning of 1965 and sold out at the end of 1977, you would have bought the S&P 500 at 86 and sold at 91, for a gain of five points (or 6 percent). In addition, you would have received an average dividend payment of about 3.5 percent per year, or about 45 percent over the 13 years, for total profit of 51 percent for the period. A 51 percent increase in 13 years is less than 4 percent annual interest (uncompounded). So if you had simply bought and held stocks for the last 13 years, you would not have matched the return of a savings account over the same period. In neither case would your returns have kept pace with the rate of inflation, but you would have done better with a compounded savings account than by staying in the market.

For people who only want to preserve their capital, the strategy of buy and hold hasn't really done that well over the last 13 years. And if you are really out to win this game, the buy-and-hold strategy has actually returned less than a bank account. To win the game you have to be able to forecast the major market swings.

AN IDEAL FORECASTING SYSTEM

Remember that the buy-and-hold strategy returned 51 percent profit in 13 years. Now let's see what the ideal forecasting system would have accomplished over the same period. Since we are most interested in major market swings, let's assume that we bought and sold short at each of the times and prices shown in Table 3. How would we have done with our hypothetically perfect forecasting system? Our initial investment would have increased 232 percent over the 13 years, or about 18 percent per year after commissions, a marvelous rate of profit. Returns for those who simply sold out instead of selling short before the major downswings would have averaged 15 percent per year. This, too, is a superior rate of profit.

Of course, there will never be any *real* forecasting system which always sells out at the top of each bull market and buys in at the very bottom of every bear market. The purpose of this exercise, then, is simply to establish an ideal standard of comparison for each of our 11 predictors. Just as the 4 percent return from the buy-and-hold strategy rep-

TABLE 3
Purchases and sales with ideal forecasting (1965–1977).

Purchases	Sales
86.12 (January 1965)	93.32 (January 1966)
77.13 (October 1966)	106.48 (December 1968)
75.59 (June 1970)	118.42 (January 1973)
67.07 (December 1974)	106.50 (January 1977)
Long positions: 94 months	Total return: 118.8%
Short positions: 62 months	Total return: 112.9%
Annual return:	18.10% per year
	15.17% per year—long side only

resents a standard of mediocrity, the 18 percent return from the ideal forecasting strategy will represent our highest standard of forecasting excellence.

In summary, the very best forecasting method can be expected to return something less than 18 percent but at least more than 4 percent on your money for each of the 13 years under consideration. The closer each predictor brings us to 18 percent, the more closely our forecasting approaches the ideal. Now that we have our 11 predictors, a 4 percent standard of mediocrity (buy and hold), and an 18 percent standard of excellence (perfect forecasting), it's time to see just how accurately each predictor has forecast the 1965–1977 market averages.

Predictor 1: 90-Day Treasury Bill Yield

Tight money and higher interest rates have ended virtually all bull markets, and they will start a bear market when stocks can no longer compete with stronger government, corporate, and individual demands for limited money supplies. Investors simply will not accept 3 percent and 4 percent dividends from stocks when they can get 7 percent to

11 percent returns from secured borrowers. At some point, interest rates reach levels that drain large sums of money from the market, and stock prices decline. Conversely, lower interest rates attract money to the market, and stock prices advance.

While this may pass as a very general explanation of the relationship between interest rates and stock prices, the two pertinent questions are which interest indicator is best used for market forecasting and what specific rate has provided the most profitable dividing line between bullish and bearish stock forecasts. There is evidence that rate changes in 90-day treasury bills lead the other short-term interest indicators by a month or so. T-bills are thus the best series for market forecasting. The most profitable interest rate for forecasting the 1965–1977 market is 6 percent.

Figure 3 shows the interest payments on treasury bills for 1965–1977. (You should keep Figure 2 firmly in mind as you study Figure 3.) Note that treasuries yielded less than 6 percent in 1965, 1966, and 1967 and didn't reach 6 percent until the bull market top of December 1968. Rates then fluctuated between 6 percent and 8 percent until October 1970, just three months after the market bottomed out in July. T-bill yields remained below 6 percent until late February 1973, five weeks after the all-time high of the S&P 500. Rates remained above 6 percent until January 1975 and came down in time to catch all but the first month of the 1975–1976 bull market. Finally, treasury bills reached a 6 percent yield in August 1977, seven months after the last bull market top of January 1977. Let us summarize our two trading rules for buying and selling the market averages with treasury bills:

> BUY *when 90-day treasury bills yield less than 6 percent.*
>
> SELL *(or sell short) when 90-day treasury bills yield more than 6 percent.*

FIGURE 3.
Predictor 1: Yields on 90-day treasury bills 1965–1977.

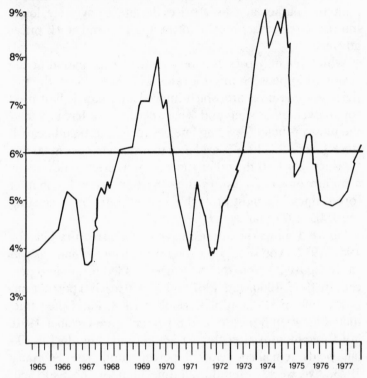

Table 4 shows that the profit from following the 6 percent trading rule for 1965–1977 would have been 131 percent, or slightly more than 10 percent per year on the initial investment. Returns would have averaged about 9 percent per year for the trader who played the long side of the market only. Both are far superior to the 4 percent returns from the simple buy-and-hold policy, but they also fall short of the ideal forecasting return of 18 percent. Altogether, the 6 percent rule on treasury bills has chalked up a good forecasting record over the last 13 years. Although the trading rule missed the 1966 market break and the 1977 market top, it has sold us out very close to the tops of two bull markets and bought us in a short time after two bear market bottoms.

Future Prospects for Predictor 1

Although the 6 percent trading rule on T-bills returned excellent profits on the market averages the last 13 years, it is important to be concerned about the arbitrary nature of the 6 percent figure. Unquestionably the general market averages and treasury yields will continue to move in opposite directions for the next several years, but this in itself provides no guarantee that 6 percent will forecast tops and bottoms in the future as well as it has done in the past. Nothing would be more short-sighted than to blindly follow a trading rule of 6 percent solely because it has worked in the past. *No indicator stands alone.* For example, the 1976 bull market topped out with treasuries at about 4.6 percent, and this is why it is essential to use additional predictors. Any single predictor might fail to forecast accurately, but it is very unlikely that all 11 indicators could fail at the same time.

With respect to specific T-bill rates and market forecasting in the next few years, it is my guess that 6 percent may be a little too high and that the player might do better with a 5 percent or 5.5 percent trading rule. Historically, interest rates were extraordinarily high from 1965 to 1978, and it is reasonable to expect somewhat lower rates in the years ahead. However, this expectation depends on three important conditions: (1) that the United States will avoid costly

TABLE 4
Purchases and sales with Predictor 1 (1965–1977).

Purchases	Sales
86.12 (January 1965)	102.04 (January 1969)
84.37 (October 1970)	112.42 (March 1973)
80.10 (February 1975)	92.49 (July 1975)
90.97 (November 1975)	97.75 (August 1977)
Long positions: 102 months	Total return: 76.0%
Short positions: 54 months	Total return: 55.8%
Annual return: 10.1% per year	
9.1% per year—long side only	

military adventures such as the Viet Nam War, (2) that the birth rate will remain low, and (3) that inflation will remain under control. If any of these three conditions are violated, I suspect that we will pay for our indulgences with higher interest rates.

Recency and Availability of Data for Predictor 1

Information on treasury bill yields is always current, and it is easily obtained. The rates are published in *The Wall Street Journal, Barron's,* most other financial publications, and many daily newspapers. Any banker or broker who is worth his salt can tell you the present yield in a minute or two. Finally, those readers who play the commodities game may be interested in speculating in treasury bill futures, which are traded on the International Monetary Market. The present margin on a contract is $1,500, and hundredths-of-a-cent changes return $25 with a daily price move limited to fifty-hundredths of a cent. This is a thin and exceptionally volatile market that offers enormous profits to players who can accurately forecast changes in short-term interest rates.

Predictor 2: Total Time Savings Deposits

In the case of Predictor 1, treasury bill yield, it was shown that the tightness of money and the extent of loan demand cause major swings in stock prices. But it is also reasonable to ask if there are other investment channels in which changing cash flows forecast changes in the market averages. Time savings deposits are one such channel. The market advances when the total of time savings deposits increases, and the market declines when time deposits decline. It is not always clear why the market averages and time deposits should rise and fall together, but it is certain that changes in time deposits usually lead changes in the market by one to several months. An indicator which tops out before the bull market tops out and which bottoms out before the bear market bot-

FIGURE 4.

Predictor 2: Total time savings deposits 1965–1977 (in millions).

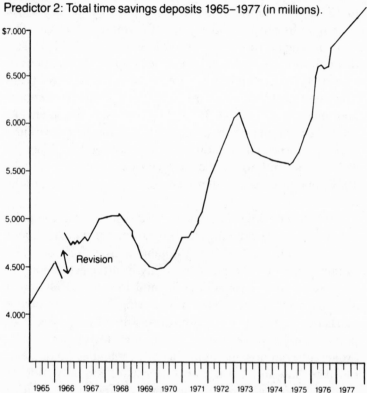

toms out might offer an extremely profitable forecasting tool.

First, let's take a look at the last 13 years of the time deposits predictor as it is shown in Figure 4. The graph shows that time deposits increased during the 1965 bull market but topped out in December 1965 before the market high of January 1966. If we allow for a revision in June 1966, time deposits bottomed out in November 1966, a single month after the 1966 bear market bottomed out. Time deposits then increased right up to the December high of the 1968 bull market, although the increase was fairly erratic during the last nine months of 1968.

Time deposits and stock prices both turned down sharply in 1969, but time deposits bottomed out in February 1970, four months ahead of the June 1970 market bottom. The two series again rose together in the second half of 1970 and through most of 1971, and then time deposits topped out in August 1972, five months before the S&P 500 reached its all-time high of 118 in January 1973. Although time deposits bottomed out in October 1973, they remained extremely low until the bear market bottomed out 12 months later. Time deposits increased rapidly in the last bull market of 1975–1976, and when the market topped out in January 1977, total time savings deposits topped out only two months later.

While it is obvious that time deposits usually lead the market averages, it is not entirely clear how the predictor should be used to obtain the most profitable market forecasts. For example, it would be possible to buy in after each monthly increase in time savings deposits and to sell (or sell short) after each monthly decline. Yet moving in and out of the market every couple of months or so will not only miss large parts of major price swings; it will also run up very costly brokerage commissions. Some better possibilities would be to calculate buy and sell signals in terms of monthly moving averages, multiple monthly moving averages, or consecutive monthly increases and decreases. There are also more complicated procedures for arriving at the trading rules which yield the most profitable trading of the market averages with time deposits, but many of these methods require fairly complicated arithmetic.

After experimenting with several different trading rules, I found that the two simple rules stated below will do just about as well for the 1965–1977 market averages as the more complicated rules.

> BUY *when the average time deposits for two consecutive months exceed the deposits at the last sell signal.*
> SELL *(or sell short) when time savings deposits decrease*

for one month and the second month's deposits fail to reverse all of the first month's decline.

How would the market player who followed these two trading rules have done in the 13 years from 1965 through 1977? Table 5 provides the answer to this question. Playing both sides of the market with our trading rules would have yielded a 13-year return of 138 percent, or 10.64 percent per year, on the original investment. The trader who played only the long side of the market would have received 9.73 percent per year, also a good return on his capital.

A Demonstration of Predictor 2

Although both trading rules have been stated as simply as possible, it would be a good idea to demonstrate their applications with some real data for stock prices and time savings deposits. Table 6 presents 30 months of data for each series, with the buy and sell signals marked on the table.

For convenience I have rounded all time deposits to the first four figures. Let's work through Table 6 on a month-

TABLE 5
Purchases and sales with Predictor 2 (1965–1977).

Purchases	Sales
86.12 (January 1965)	91.60 (April 1966)
91.43 (June 1967)	95.67 (April 1968)
100.53 (June 1968)	100.30 (July 1968)
103.76 (October 1968)	101.26 (April 1969)
75.59 (June 1970)	84.37 (October 1970)
90.05 (December 1970)	97.29 (October 1971)
99.17 (December 1971)	117.50 (December 1972)
114.62 (February 1973)	110.27 (April 1973)
104.75 (June 1973)	109.84 (October 1973)
93.45 (February 1974)	82.82 (July 1974)
67.07 (December 1974)	88.57 (October 1975)
88.70 (December 1975)	100.18 (July 1977)

Long positions: 98 months	Total return: 79.5%
Short positions: 58 months	Total return: 58.8%

Annual return: 10.64% per year
9.73% per year—long side only

TABLE 6
Demonstration of buy and sell signals with Predictor 2
(30 months).

Date	Stock Prices	Time Deposits	Date	Stock Prices	Time Deposits
Aug. (1972)	110.01	$5,983 million	Nov.	102.03	$5,628 million
Sept.	109.39	5,807	Dec.	94.78	5,709 (BUY)
Oct.	109.56	5,811 (SELL)	Jan. (1974)	96.11	5,680
Nov.	115.05	5,818	Feb.	93.45	5,714
Dec.	117.50	5,857 (BUY)	March	97.44	5,848
Jan. (1973)	118.42	5,801	April	92.46	5,783
Feb.	114.62	5,797 (SELL)	May	89.67	5,787 (SELL)
March	112.42	5,847	June	89.79	5,811
April	110.27	5,796 (BUY)	July	82.82	5,760
May	107.22	5,822	Aug.	76.03	5,708
June	104.75	5,825	Sept.	68.12	5,722
July	105.83	5,735	Oct.	69.44	5,741 (BUY)
Aug.	103.80	5,629 (SELL)	Nov.	71.74	5,781
Sept.	105.61	5,617	Dec.	67.07	5,848
Oct.	109.84	5,613	Jan. (1975)	72.56	5,874

by-month basis. We start with time deposits reaching a new high of $5,983 million in August 1972, but deposits declined to $5,807 million in September. A single monthly decline might be a sign that stock prices are heading downward, or it could simply be an insignificant fluctuation in time deposits. That's why the sell signal from our trading rules requires a monthly decline that is followed by a failure to erase that decline in the next month. By the end of October the answer is clear: deposits increased from $5,807 million to $5,811 million but they did not return to the August level of $5,983 million. While the sell signal appears at the end of October, data for time deposits are published five to six weeks late, which means that we would have reached the first or second week of December 1972 before the October deposits were available. We would have sold out for 117.50 in December (see Table 5). All other transactions are also calculated for the market averages two months behind the actual buy and sell signals.

November deposits were up to $5,818 million from $5,811

million and December deposits increased to $5,857 million. Our trading rule says to buy when the average deposits of two consecutive months exceed the deposits for the last sell signal. The average of $5,818 million (November) and $5,857 million (December) is $5,837.5 million. Since this is higher than $5,811 million (October), there's a buy signal at the end of December on which we act in February 1973.

January 1973 deposits are $5,801 million, a drop from December's $5,857 million, and February drops to $5,797 million, thus triggering another sell signal at the end of February 1973. The average of the March and April deposits exceeds the February deposits, so we get a buy signal at the end of April. May and June deposits increase, but July's deposits drop to $5,735 million from June's $5,825 million. So there is another sell signal when August (5,629) deposits fail to reach $5,825 million.

The sell signal remains in force for September and October, but deposits turn upward again in November. Although we sold out in August (5,629), the last sell signal was in October (5,613). So the November and December average need only exceed October's deposits for a buy signal to be given. In fact, the November–December average surpassed both August and October, so we have a buy signal at the end of 1973.

Deposits drop from $5,709 million to $5,680 million in January 1974, but February deposits rebound past $5,709 million to $5,714 million, and no sell signal is given. However, the April decline was followed by a failure of May's deposits to return to March's level, another sell signal. The sell signal at the end of May was followed by another sell signal at the end of August (5,708), but the average of deposits for September and October (5,731.5) surpassed the August deposits, and we bought back into the market at 67.07 in December 1974.

The last six rows of Table 5 summarize the transactions conducted during our 30-month demonstration. The record looks very promising. The time deposits predictor sold us out a single month before the top of the greatest bull market in history. The predictor then chalked up a very minor four-point loss in early 1973 and a five-point gain in the middle of 1973. We then took an 11-point loss in the first half of 1974, but time deposits bought us back in at the very bottom of the worst bear market since 1937. Thus, while the market dropped 51 points in less than two years, we lost only 10 points (less than 20 percent of the decline) during the bear swing. No indicator is perfect, and no indicator stands alone, but Predictor 2 has shown enough forecasting power to keep the market player out of serious trouble during major bear swings. It may help keep you out of trouble in future market cycles.

Future Prospects for Predictor 2

The relationship between total time savings deposits and the stock market average is probably less dependable than the relationship between T-bill yields (Predictor 1) and the market averages. The reason for placing less faith in time deposits than in yields on treasury bills is because the first relationship is merely correlational, while the second relationship may be causal. When the federal government increases or decreases the interest rate on T-bills by as little as a single point, billions and tens of billions of dollars are taken from or restored to circulation in the general economy. The effect on the stock market is direct, obvious, and reasonably certain. The case of total time savings deposits is much different, however. From a bull market top to a bear market bottom, time deposits may decline by only $2 billion or $3 billion. But total losses in stock values easily run to $200 billion and $300 billion in major bear markets. Thus, there is no chance that cash flows into and out of time savings accounts can have any direct effect on the market averages. All that can be stated with certainty is that changes in time deposits have consistently led changes in the 1965–1977 market averages, and that nobody can really explain why.

The alert market player should develop an awareness of conditions that might distort the forecasting power of total time savings deposits in the future. For example, time savings accounts must compete for money against corporate and federal bonds, large certificates of deposit, and several other intermediate-term investment opportunities. Hence, sudden and pronounced swings in time deposits might result from new discrepancies among various interest rates, and the market forecasting power of Predictor 2 might be distorted or eliminated.

Finally, while our two specific trading rules for playing the market with time deposits worked out well, this provides no assurance that some other trading rules won't forecast more accurately in the future. Moving monthly averages, percentage changes, consecutive advances and declines—all offer the arithmetically oriented reader the opportunity to develop his own trading rules for future market cycles. For the reader who wants to try his hand at devising his own trading rules from previous data, I have included 13 years (156 months) of market averages and time deposits in the Appendix at the end of the book.

Recency and Availability of Data for Predictor 2

Total time savings deposits are reported about five weeks after the end of the last month for which figures are available. The market player will thus be acting on data which are six to seven weeks old. I do not know of any way to obtain this information any sooner, and I don't think the delay makes much difference for a series of market cycles. No indicator ever catches the exact top of all bull markets or the exact bottom of all bear markets, and the short delay in the reporting of time deposits shouldn't make a great difference in the long run.

Total monthly time savings deposits are sometimes reported in *Barron's, The Wall Street Journal,* and other financial papers. The monthly changes are always reported in two separate monthly publications of the U.S. Department of

Commerce: *Survey of Current Business* and *Business Conditions Digest*. Virtually all large and medium-size libraries subscribe to the monthly *Survey of Current Business*, and the periodical can also be found in many smaller libraries.

Predictor 3: Authorized Housing Permits

The number of permits issued for the construction of single-family houses is one of the most useful forecasters of changes in the market averages. The reason for this is that changes in housing permits run so far ahead of the U.S. business cycle that they also lead stock prices by a few months. The best explanation of this relationship is that the availability of money is reflected in home construction planning before it affects stock prices. So let's take a look at housing permits for 1965 through 1977 (Figure 5).

The number of housing permits increased throughout 1965 and topped out in December, one month before the January 1966 market top. Permits then turned down and bottomed out in October, the same month as the 1966 market bottom. Housing permits rose sharply in the first year of the next bull market (1967) and leveled off in 1968, as the market average continued its advance. Permits finally topped out in September 1968, three months before the bull market peaked in December 1968. Both series declined in 1969, but housing permits bottomed out in January 1970, four months before the market lows of May 1970. Permits and the market both turned up through the next bull swing (1971–1972), and once again permits topped out (October 1972) a few months before the market reached its all-time high in January 1973. The decline in permits consistently led the 1973–1974 bear market losses, but housing permits missed the last bull market (1975–1976) by a month. The market average turned up in January 1975, and housing permits turned up one month later. The two series rose together through the entire bull market of 1975–1976, and

FIGURE 5.

Predictor 3: Authorized housing permits 1965–1977.

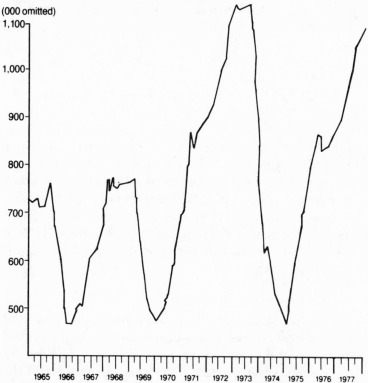

when the market topped out in January 1977, housing permits topped out only two months later.

Although it is clear that housing permits lead the market averages, we again have the problem of developing specific trading rules to exploit this general relationship most profitably. To buy in or sell out after each monthly advance or decline in housing permits would yield nothing but small profits for the market player and large commissions for his broker. Trading rules similar to the rules we developed for total time deposits don't forecast the market very accurately when they are applied to housing permits.

After experimenting with several fairly complicated trading rules, I found that substantial profits could also be obtained from rules which use consecutive advances and declines in Predictor 3:

> BUY *when monthly housing permits increase for three consecutive months.*
>
> SELL (*or sell short*) *when monthly housing permits decline for three consecutive months.*

Table 7 shows the profits that would have been obtained by the player who followed these trading rules from 1965 through 1977. Total returns for the 13-year period would have been 98.2 percent, or 7.55 percent per year. Annual returns would have averaged 9.03 percent for the player who confined himself to the long side of the market. Table 8 presents a 16-month demonstration of buy and sell signals for housing permits.

Future Prospects for Predictor 3

In evaluating the role of housing permits as forecasters of future market averages, it is most important to understand the nature of this relationship. Only then can we understand circumstances which might distort market forecasts in the future. One contingency to bear in mind is that during the 13 years under study (1965–1977) the financing of single-family housing was transacted mostly through private lenders. At other times in the past, and possibly in the future, the federal government and other public agencies have been more directly involved in the financing of housing, and this could alter the relationship between housing permits and the market averages, especially if cheaper public funds are allocated for construction financing. In general, the alert market player should be wary of any circumstances which might loosen loan money for housing from dependency on general interest rates.

There are also changes in other conditions which may af-

TABLE 7
Purchases and sales with Predictor 3
(1965–1977).

Purchases	Sales
86.12 (January 1965)	85.04 (June 1965)
89.42 (March 1967)	100.30 (July 1968)
105.40 (November 1968)	101.26 (April 1969)
77.92 (August 1970)	107.22 (May 1973)
85.71 (August 1975)	99.05 (April 1977)
Long positions: 80 months	Total return: 60.2%
Short positions: 76 months	Total return: 38.0%
Annual return: 7.55% per year	
9.03% per year—long side only	

TABLE 8
Demonstration of buy and sell signals with
Predictor 3 (16 months).

	Stock Prices	Housing Permits (in thousands)
Feb. (1968)	90.75	720
March	89.09	687
April	95.67	672
May	97.87	667
June	100.53	655
July	100.30	688 SELL
August	98.11	700
Sept.	101.34	732
Oct.	103.76	714
Nov.	105.40	731 BUY
Dec.	106.48	709
Jan. (1969)	102.04	687
Feb.	101.46	679
March	99.30	660
April	101.26	656 SELL
May	104.62	639

fect the demand for new single-family housing. For example, lower birth rates and the increasing childlessness of more marriages might affect the demand for housing. Or if the tax privileges of home ownership were extended to renters, the relationship between housing permits and market action might be altered.

Here are examples of two additional contingencies to keep in mind when playing the market using housing permits. Although housing permits are a seasonally adjusted series, an unusually severe winter could depress housing starts for two or three months and cause the player to be unduly pessimistic in his market forecasting. Conversely, an unseasonably mild winter might increase permits and entrap the player in an overly optimistic market forecast for the spring and summer ahead. One final example. In addition to the availability of financing, labor disturbances play an important role in housing plans. Strikes and other work stoppages are sufficiently frequent in the construction industry to affect private building plans.

These are only a few of the possibilities that might alter the relationship between changes in housing permits and major market swings. My own opinion is that housing permits will continue to provide fairly accurate market forecasts in the years ahead. But I do not trust the forecasting stability of housing permits as much as I trust T-bills (Predictor 1).

As with T-bills and time deposits, I have included 13 years of housing permits in the Appendix. The reader who wants to experiment with a variety of different trading rules should break out his pencil and paper and see how several additional trading rules compare with my rules.

Since housing permits rise sharply in the first half of a bull market and then level off very quickly in the second half, the player needs a fairly loose trading rule to avoid selling out on small downward fluctuations in maturing bull markets. So it's important to be certain that permits have clearly turned down before switching sides in the market. With this predictor it's probably better to risk acting a little late than acting too early, and this is doubly true for the player who plans to short the market on the downswing. Housing permits, like time deposits, are reported about a month late.

Recency and Availability of Data for Predictor 3

Housing permits are one of the 12 leading indicators reported monthly by the National Bureau of Economic Research. All 12 indicators are reported a month late, and occasional adjustments (usually quite minor) may appear in the NBER indicators a month or two after the first report. *The Wall Street Journal, Barron's,* other financial papers, and the better daily newspapers discuss monthly changes in housing permits along with the other NBER leading indicators. Sometimes these publications report specific numbers of permits issued during the previous month. When they do not, the exact number of permits can be obtained from one of three federal publications: *Economic Indicators, Survey of Current Business,* or *Business Conditions Digest.* Even the smallest public library will usually subscribe to at least one of these monthly publications.

Predictor 4: Brokers' Cash Accounts

Predictor 4 may seem a little obvious. But if it's obvious to you and me, it certainly isn't obvious to the "professionals" of Wall Street, the fellows who will lose your money by playing the market with odd lots and confidence indexes rather than save your money with a predictor which has been sitting right under their noses for over 40 years. The logic underlying Predictor 4 isn't too hard to follow. When the total of brokers' cash accounts increases, there is money to go around. A short time later this money flows into equities, and the market averages advance. Just the opposite effect occurs when there is a decrease in brokers' cash accounts: money grows tight, it leaves the market, and the S&P 500 declines.

Figure 6 tells the story of brokers' cash accounts in the 13 years from 1965 through 1977. Cash accounts rose with the 1965 bull market and topped out in April 1966, two months after the beginning of the 1966 market break. Cash accounts

FIGURE 6.
Predictor 4: Brokers' cash accounts 1965–1977 (in millions).

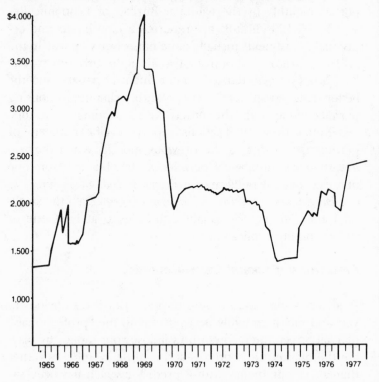

and the market then declined together in 1966, and brokers' cash accounts bottomed out in October, the same month the market saw its 1966 low.

With cash accounts showing the way, both series rose throughout 1967. Accounts then fluctuated during the first half of 1968, and the market price action was erratic for the same period. Both took off again later in 1968 and topped out together in December of that year.

Accounts and the market declined in the 1969–1970 bear market, and accounts bottomed out in June 1970, a couple of months before the first swing of the next bull market. Accounts increased again until March 1971, topping out a month before the beginning of the short 1971 market break. This time cash accounts hit bottom in September, and the market was on its way back up in December 1971. Cash accounts forecast erratically in 1972, the last year of our greatest bull market. Accounts actually topped out in February 1972, at $2,108 million, but they ran just below their top and recovered to $1,957 million in December 1972, the last month of the bull market.

In the first year of the 1973–1974 bear market, the decline in cash accounts ran a little behind the market, but the predictor eventually caught up with the 1974 market. Cash accounts bottomed out in September 1974, and the market bottomed out three months later, right on schedule. Cash accounts and the market average increased together in both years of the most recent 1975–1976 bull market, and both series topped out in January 1977.

As with the first three predictors, our problem is to develop the most profitable trading index for playing the market averages with cash accounts. Once again, monthly purchases and sales of the market following monthly advances and declines in cash accounts are going to make a lot more money for our stockbroker than they will ever make for us. After searching for two fairly uncomplicated trading rules which will enable the player to forecast the 1965–1977 market averages with brokers' cash accounts, I found the following:

> BUY *when the two most recent months of brokers' cash accounts are greater than the accounts of the two previous months.*
>
> SELL *(or sell short) when the two most recent months of brokers' cash accounts are lower than the accounts of the two previous months.*

Table 9 shows the profits that would have accrued to the investor who played the market with these trading rules from 1965 through 1977. Profits would have totaled 128.3 percent, or 9.87 percent per year. For playing the long side

TABLE 9
Purchases and sales with Predictor 4
(1965–1977).

Purchases	Sales
86.12 (January 1965)	89.28 (May 1965)
85.04 (June 1965)	86.49 (August 1965)
89.38 (September 1965)	91.60 (April 1966)
86.06 (June 1966)	85.84 (July 1966)
81.33 (December 1966)	89.09 (March 1968)
97.87 (May 1968)	98.11 (August 1968)
103.76 (October 1968)	99.30 (March 1969)
96.21 (November 1969)	87.16 (February 1970)
77.92 (August 1970)	97.11 (February 1971)
99.60 (March 1971)	101.64 (May 1971)
99.17 (December 1971)	108.81 (April 1972)
109.56 (October 1972)	114.62 (February 1973)
105.61 (September 1973)	96.11 (January 1974)
69.44 (October 1974)	92.49 (July 1975)
90.07 (November 1975)	101.93 (April 1976)
101.16 (June 1976)	99.05 (April 1977)
97.75 (July 1977)	93.74 (October 1977)

Long positions:	75 months	Total return:	75.1%
Short positions:	81 months	Total return:	53.2%

Annual return: 9.87% per year
12.02% per year—long side only

of the market only, returns would have averaged 12.02 percent per year.

Since I want to make the use of these trading rules as clear as possible, a brief demonstration of Predictor 4 might be helpful. Table 10 shows 29 months of data for stock prices, brokers' cash accounts, the two most recent months of cash accounts, and the two months of cash accounts previous to the recent months. The table also shows each buy and sell signal that follows from our trading rules for playing the market with cash accounts.

The table begins in July 1972. Cash accounts for July were $1,733 million, and they were $1,845 million for the month before that. Thus, cash accounts for the two most recent months (June and July) were 1,733 + 1,845 = $3,578 million. Cash accounts for April and May 1972 totaled $3,960 million. Since the recent months' total of $3,578 million was less than the previous two months' total of $3,960 million, the last sell signal remains in force. It was the same story for August and September 1972: total accounts for the two most recent months remained below the total for the two previous months. Finally, in October 1972 the accounts for the two

TABLE 10
Demonstration of buy and sell signals with Predictor 4 (29 months).

	Stock Prices	Cash Accounts (in millions)	Two Most Recent Months (in millions)	Two Previous Months (in millions)
July (1972)	107.21	$1,733	$3,578	$3,960
August	111.01	1,677	3,410	3,785
Sept.	109.39	1,708	3,385	3,578
Oct.	109.56 BUY	1,842	3,550	3,410
Nov.	115.05	1,828	3,670	3,385
Dec.	117.50	1,957	3,785	3,550
Jan. (1973)	118.42	1,883	3,840	3,670
Feb.	114.62 SELL	1,770	3,653	3,785
March	112.42	1,719	3,499	3,840
April	110.27	1,536	3,255	3,653
May	107.22	1,564	3,100	3,499
June	104.75	1,472	3,036	3,255
July	105.83	1,542	3,014	3,100
August	103.80	1,462	3,004	3,036
Sept.	105.61 BUY	1,632	3,094	3,014
Oct.	109.84	1,713	3,345	3,004
Nov.	102.03	1,685	3,398	3,094
Dec.	94.78	1,700	3,385	3,345
Jan. (1974)	96.11 SELL	1,666	3,366	3,398
Feb.	93.45	1,604	3,270	3,385
March	97.44	1,583	3,187	3,366
April	92.46	1,440	3,023	3,270
May	89.67	1,420	2,860	3,187
June	89.79	1,360	2,780	3,023
July	82.82	1,391	2,751	2,860
August	76.03	1,382	2,773	2,780
Sept.	68.12	1,354	2,736	2,751
Oct.	69.44 BUY	1,419	2,773	2,773
Nov.	71.74	1,447	2,866	2,736

recent months (3,550) rose above the previous two months' accounts (3,410). This was a buy signal.

Since cash accounts are reported currently, the market player would have bought while the S&P 500 was at 109.56 in October. Recent cash accounts remained above previous accounts through November (3,670 vs. 3,385) and December (3,785 vs. 3,550) of 1972, and also through January 1973, the month the greatest bull market topped out. In February 1973, one month later, recent accounts dropped below previous accounts, and the player would have sold out (or sold short) at 114.62.

The February 1973 sell signal remained in force through August 1973, but in September, recent accounts rose above previous accounts, and a buy signal would have brought the player back into the bear market at 105.61. The September 1973 buy signal lasted until the sell signal of January 1974, and the player would have sold out and gone short at 96.11. This last sell signal remained in force through September 1974, but recent accounts pulled even with previous accounts in October 1974. The player would have bought back in at 69.44 in October, just before the bear market ended and only three months before the 1975–1976 bull market got under way.

From this brief demonstration it is clear that cash accounts are a profitable market forecaster. The player was sold out a single month after the top of the greatest bull market in history. Then, while the 1973–1974 bear market skidded from 118 to 67, the player was caught with only a nine-point loss on one false buy signal between October 1973 and January 1974. Finally, the player bought back in at 69, just two points from the December 1974 market bottom. The player who sold short in addition to selling out at each sell signal would have taken enormous profits from the 1973–1974 bear market.

It is once again necessary to repeat two important points: one, no indicator forecasts perfectly, and two, no indicator stands alone. Brokers' cash accounts were an excellent tool for forecasting changes in the stock market averages between 1965 and 1978, but cash accounts will not work every time, and they should always be used in conjunction with the other major market indicators.

Future Prospects for Predictor 4

Like treasury bills, brokers' cash accounts may enjoy a long future as a successful forecaster of stock market averages. I expect that Predictor 4 will be a more stable and reliable forecaster in the future than either time deposits or housing permits. For one thing, the relationship between cash accounts and market averages is immediate and direct. When brokers are carrying large cash balances on their books, economic conditions are good and business attitudes are optimistic. Before long, these cash balances and a lot of additional money from the general economy are going to drive up stock prices. When cash accounts turn down, they are one of the earliest signals of tighter money ahead, and the market turns down a few months later.

Comparatively small changes in brokers' cash accounts precede much larger changes in the market. For example, cash accounts declined by only a half a billion dollars in the 1973–1974 bear market, while stocks lost about $400 billion of value in the same market. Clearly, this is not a cause-and-effect relationship. Cash accounts indicate in which direction much larger amounts of money will move in the future, but actual changes in cash accounts are not large enough for any direct impact on the market.

While I think it unlikely that the cash accounts will be distorted as a future market indicator, there is one change that may affect the actual size of brokers' cash accounts. The player with a cash balance at a brokerage house collects no interest on his money, but this may soon be changing. It is now possible to transfer this cash to special bank accounts which pay daily interest until the player reinvests in the market. If this practice becomes widespread, the total of cash accounts will be lowered. Except for the first few months, however, this would not distort the forecasting accuracy of the cash accounts indicator.

A final word on our two trading rules. Brokers' cash accounts comprise a series that shows many small reversals on a month-to-month basis. The player who uses only the previous month's accounts will be buying or selling as often as eight or nine times a year. Brokerage commissions make it nearly impossible to trade this often and still come out ahead. Therefore, profitable trading rules must involve a comparison of two or more recent months to previous months. Our rule of comparing the two most recent months against the two previous months worked out profitably, but 34 transactions in 156 months requires more trading than I can honestly recommend. For players who want to develop their own trading rules, I have listed 13 years (1965–1977) of brokers' cash accounts in the Appendix.

Recency and Availability of Data for Predictor 4

Values for brokers' cash accounts are published in the *Survey of Current Business*, which is available at most public libraries. However, the *Survey* publishes cash accounts several months late. The market laboratory section of *Barron's* publishes current values of brokers' cash accounts, as do a few other financial papers, and these are the best sources because the player needs the earliest information he can obtain for this predictor. Virtually all public libraries subscribe to weekly issues of *Barron's*.

Predictor 5: Stock Exchange Call Loan Interest Rate

Many speculators and some investors borrow money in order to increase the amounts of their market purchases. To provide a simple example of playing the market with borrowed money, let us consider the case of the player who has $1,000 and wants to buy a stock quoted at $10 per share. If we ignore commissions, the player's $1,000 will buy 100 shares. Now assume that the stock advances to $15 per share. If the player sells at 15, he receives $1,500 for his original $1,000 investment, or a profit of $500.

However, there is a second and more risky choice open to the player. He can take his $1,000, borrow an additional $1,000 from a brokerage firm, and then buy 200 instead of 100 shares of the same stock at $10. Now if the stock goes to 15, the player will sell out for $3,000. After he returns the $1,000 loan plus interest to the brokerage house and deducts his original $1,000, the player will have a profit of nearly $1,000, or just about twice his $500 profit from trading with only his own money. Of course, the leverage of borrowed money works both ways. The player doubles his profits if he forecasts correctly, but he doubles his losses if he borrows and the stock goes down.

The point of this example is neither to encourage nor to discourage playing the market with borrowed money. Rather, it is to introduce the stock exchange call loan rate. Interest is charged on money that is borrowed to play the market, and this interest rate turns out to be an important indicator of future stock market changes.

Figure 7 shows the call loan interest rate from 1965 to 1978. In 1965, the last year of a bull market, the loan interest rate varied between 4.5 percent and 4.75 percent. The rate rose to 4.9 percent in December 1965, and it stood at 5.07 percent when the bull market topped out in January 1966. The call loan interest rate continued its rise through the 1966 market break, and it topped out at 6.25 percent in the last four months of 1966. The market also bottomed out in October 1966.

The rate dropped to 6.2 percent in January 1967, and as the first year of the 1967–1968 bull market progressed, the call loan rate declined to 5.50 percent. The rate returned to 6 percent in early 1968 and then fluctuated between 6.18 percent and 6.5 percent for the rest of the year. The loan rate stood at 6.5 percent when the bull market topped out in December 1968. The interest rate increased from 6.97 percent to 8.5 percent through the 1969 bear market, but it fi-

FIGURE 7.
Predictor 5: Stock exchange call loan interest rate 1965–1977.

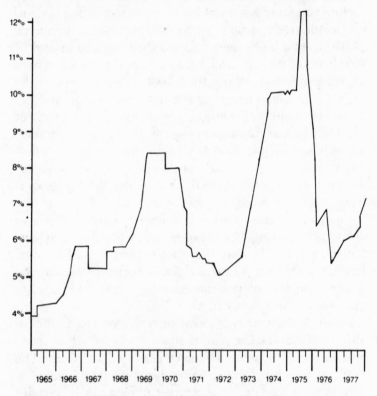

nally turned down to 8.4 percent (March 1970) and 8 percent (April 1970) as the bear market ended.

The next bull swing, which started in September 1970, saw the loan rate decline from 7.90 percent to 5.49 percent by July 1971. The rate then increased suddenly to 6.00 percent for two months and then declined to a low of 4.55 percent in March 1972. The market continued upward through the rest of 1972, and the loan rate stood at 5.75 percent by the year's end.

When our greatest bull market topped out in January 1973, the loan rate was 6.01 percent. By December 1973, the market had lost 24 points, and the interest rate had worked its way from 6.01 percent to 10 percent. 1974 was the worst year in recent market history, and the loan rate increased from 9.95 percent to an incredible 12.25 percent (September 1974) before the year ended. Call loan rates stood at 10.5 percent by the end of 1974, but they had clearly turned down before the start of the 1975 bull market. The rates continued to drop quickly (10.11 percent, 9.02 percent, 8.09 percent, and 7.66 percent) in the first four months of the 1975 bull market. Rates then remained within a range of 6.88 percent–8.22 percent as the bull market continued through 1976. When the last bull market topped out in January 1977, the call loan rate stood at 7.5 percent, and the rate rose to 9.25 percent shortly before the end of 1977.

There is clearly a strong and consistent relationship between the stock exchange call loan rate and the market averages. When the loan interest rate increases, the market declines; when the loan rate declines, the market advances. This reasoning applies especially well to bear markets, because the next bull market never starts until the loan interest rate has topped out.

The next task is to develop trading rules that most profitably exploit the market forecasting power of Predicator 5. Once again I explored several possibilities in order to develop the simplest and most profitable trading rules. Here they are:

> BUY *when the call loan interest rate declines more than .3 percent in any month.*
>
> SELL (*or sell short*) *when the call loan interest rate shows three consecutive monthly increases.*

Table 11 shows the profits that would have resulted from playing the market with our trading rules from 1965 through 1977. Playing both sides of the market would have yielded a 13-year return of 121.4 percent, or 9.34 percent per year. Profits averaged 9.51 percent per year for the player who restricted himself to the long side of the market.

TABLE 11
Purchases and sales with Predictor 5
(1965–1977).

Purchases	Sales
86.12 (January 1965)	91.73 (December 1965)
87.36 (February 1967)	95.67 (April 1968)
85.95 (April 1970)	107.21 (July 1972)
93.45 (February 1974)	89.79 (June 1974)
69.44 (October 1974)	84.67 (September 1975)
90.07 (November 1975)	97.75 (August 1977)

Long positions: 89 months	Total return: 70.5%
Short positions: 67 months	Total return: 50.9%

Annual return: 9.34% per year
9.51% per year—long side only

Since I want to make both trading rules clearly under-stood, Table 12 presents a brief demonstration of playing the market averages with the stock exchange call loan inter-est rate. The table begins with February 1972 with the last buy signal (April 1970) still in force, and the loan rate of 4.63 percent. In March the rate dropped to 4.55 percent, but increased to 4.88 percent in April. That's one increase. The May rate jumped to 5 percent for two consecutive in-creases. June 1972 was unchanged from May, but the July rate went to 5.23 percent. That made three consecutive in-creases in the loan rate, so we sold out (or sold short) in July at 107.21. The rate increased further in August, again in October 1972, and once again in November, closing out 1972 at 5.75 percent. Six consecutive advances in 1972 loan rates was an almost certain sign of trouble for the 1973 mar-ket. The rate stood at 6.01 percent when the bull market topped out in January 1973. The loan interest rate then made eight consecutive advances to September as the 1973 market fell apart. Finally, in October 1973 the rate eased from 10.04 percent to 10.02 percent. The small decline of .02 percent was probably a change fluctuation, which is the reason why our trading rule requires a decline of at least .3 percent before we buy in.

From November 1973 to January 1974, rates eased to 9.95 percent, but it wasn't until February's decline, 9.95 percent to 9.39 percent, that we bought back into the market at 93.45. The interest rate dropped again in March 1974, but April (10.23 percent), May (11.48 percent), and June (11.78 percent) scored three consecutive advances. We sold out of the bear market in June 1974 at 89.79, with a small loss of 3.66 points. The rate continued to climb through July, August, and September. Finally in October 1974, at the bottom of the bear market, the rate dropped from 12.25 percent to 11.8 percent, so we bought in three months before the 1975–1976 bull market got under way.

TABLE 12
Demonstration of buy and sell signals with Predictor 5 (36 months).

Month	Stock Prices	Call Loan Interest Rate	Month	Stock Prices	Call Loan Interest Rate
Feb. (1972)	105.24	4.63%	August	103.80	9.41%
March	107.69	4.55	Sept.	105.61	10.04
April	108.81	4.88	Oct.	109.84	10.02
May	107.65	5.00	Nov.	102.03	10.00
June	108.01	5.00	Dec.	94.78	10.00
July	107.21 SELL	5.23	Jan. (1974)	96.11	9.95
August	111.01	5.25	Feb.	93.45 BUY	9.39
Sept.	109.39	5.25	March	97.44	9.08
Oct.	109.56	5.70	April	92.46	10.23
Nov.	115.05	5.75	May	89.67	11.48
Dec.	117.50	5.75	June	89.79 SELL	11.78
Jan. (1973)	118.42	6.01	July	82.82	12.22
Feb.	114.62	6.29	August	76.03	12.25
March	112.42	6.80	Sept.	68.12	12.25
April	110.27	7.00	Oct.	69.44 BUY	11.80
May	107.22	7.18	Nov.	71.14	10.80
June	104.75	7.83	Dec.	67.07	10.50
July	105.83	8.41	Jan. (1975)	72.56	10.11

As is apparent from our demonstration, Predictor 5 does a good job of market forecasting. It sold us out a few months before the top of the 1972 bull market, returned huge profits for the short sellers through the 1973–1974 bear market, and then brought us back into the market only three months before the beginning of the 1975–1976 bull market swing.

Future Prospects for Predictor 5

It seems very unlikely that the general forecasting power of the call loan interest rate will be distorted in the years ahead. The loan interest rate has successfully forecast major market tops and bottoms since the Great Crash of 1929, and it's a safe bet that Predictor 5 will continue to forecast well in the future. When there is surplus loan money to buy stocks, there is much additional money in the general economy that is also moving toward the market. When loan money grows tight, the call loan rate increases, and large pools of money soon move away from stocks and into other investment media. In sum, the relationship between call loan rates and stock prices is quite straightforward, suggesting that the forecasting power of Predicator 5 arises from its capacity to indicate whether large amounts of money will be moving to or from the market a month or so later.

With respect to our specific trading rules, the alert market player should be aware that changes in the loan rate have a strong tendency to continue and only weak tendencies to reverse themselves. This is the reason why a buy rule could be developed around a single monthly decline greater than .3 percent. There are many other profitable trading rules for playing the market with call loan rates, but all successful trading rules for Predictor 5 will show one common element: they wait for the start of a definite trend in the call loan interest rate before producing a buy or sell signal. The Appendix provides 13 years of call loan interest rates for the player who wants to experiment with his own trading rules for Predictor 5.

Recency and Availability of Data for Predictor 5

The *Survey of Current Business* published the stock exchange call loan rate on a monthly basis through 1976, but this series was discontinued in 1977. Since prompt action is important with Predictor 5, the player needs the most recent information he can obtain. *The Wall Street Journal, Barron's*, and many other financial papers publish the call loan rate on a periodic basis. A telephone call to any major brokerage firm will also provide the present stock exchange call loan rate.

Predictor 6: True Weekly Earnings

The relationship of stock market prices to inflation is always a controversial issue. Some authorities believe that stocks are an excellent hedge against inflation, others believe that inflation drives stock prices down, and still other experts argue that inflation has different effects on different stocks. In fact, each view of inflation and the stock market has been correct at different times.

For example, stock prices rose with inflation in the 1930s, 1940s, and 1950s. Through most of the 1960s inflation had no general effect on the market. However, in the 1970s the worst bear markets have followed the largest inflations in the U.S. economy. Finally, as common sense might suggest, there is impressive evidence that inflation does not affect all companies equally. Stocks of banks, loan companies, larger retail merchandisers, and other corporations that extend loans and credit usually take an especially severe beating during periods of higher inflation. On the other hand, stocks of companies that are primarily borrowers rather than lenders (for example, steel, chemicals, drugs) seem to fare somewhat better during periods of higher inflation.

While the overall relationship between inflation and stock prices is extremely complex, there is one specific feature of this relationship that is reliable enough to provide accurate market forecasting. This is the historical relationship between the real wages of nonagricultural workers and the market averages. Nonagricultural workers comprise the largest segment of the U.S. labor force, and if the economy is to remain prosperous, these workers must be able to purchase the goods and services they produce. Therefore, when wages are increasing faster than the rate of inflation, workers will enjoy increased purchasing power. But when overall wage increases lag behind inflation, the worker's purchasing power is decreased. Not surprisingly, these increases and decreases in purchasing power provide an excellent leading indicator of changes in the stock market averages in the months ahead.

Having explained Predictor 6 to this point, I next want to describe the specific indicator of workers' purchasing power that is most useful for market forecasting. Spendable weekly wages is an especially useful forecasting index because it measures take-home pay after deductions for federal and state income taxes, Social Security, and other taxes. Thus, spendable earnings are perhaps the best indicator of the money available to purchase goods and services from the general economy. Now let's look at the last 13 years (1965–1977) of spendable weekly earnings (corrected for inflation) and compare them with the rise and fall of the market averages over the same period of time. Figure 8 shows that real earnings increased through 1965 and topped out in February 1966, one month after the end of the bull market. Real earnings then declined through the 1966 market break and bottomed out one month before the end of the bear market in October 1966.

Earnings also increased through the bull market of 1967–1968, and they finally topped out at $92.85 per week in September 1968. Three months later the 1967–1968 bull market topped out at its December high of 106.48. As expected, declining spendable earnings also led the 1969–1970 bear market. Earnings finally hit bottom at $89.11 per week in April 1970, and the bear market bottomed out two months later in June.

FIGURE 8.

Predictor 6: Weekly spendable earnings per employed worker 1965–1977 (in constant dollars).

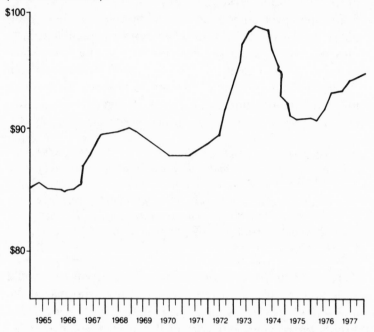

In the 1971–1972 bull swing, real earnings once again led the market. When weekly earnings finally topped out at $97.79 in October 1972, the bull market came to end in January 1973, only three months later. Declining spendable earnings also led most of the 1973–1974 bear market. However, inflation was so severe in the last half of 1974 that the next bull market got under way before workers' real earnings could catch up with inflation. In this case, the bear market finally bottomed out in December 1974, while real earnings didn't hit bottom until March 1975. Although earnings missed the beginning of the last bull market by three months, the predictor quickly recovered and increased with market averages through the rest of 1975 and most of 1976. Earnings topped out in November 1976, two months before the top of the last bull market. Finally, real earnings declined with the S&P 500 through the first half of 1977, but they advanced quite unexpectedly through the second half of the 1977 bear market.

Our next problem is to devise trading rules that most profitably exploit this relationship between real spendable earnings and the stock market averages. Among the several possibilities for trading rules, the best would be buy and sell signals that ignore minor fluctuations in true weekly earnings while responding to the major changes. Here are two trading rules that meet both of these requirements:

> BUY *when spendable weekly earnings increase by $1.00 or more for any month OR when earnings increase by 40¢ for each of two consecutive months.*

> SELL (*or sell short) when spendable weekly earnings decrease by $1.00 or more for any month OR when earnings decrease by 40¢ for each of two consecutive months.*

Table 13 shows the transactions and the profits that would have accrued to the investor or speculator who played the 1965–1977 market averages with these two trading rules. Profits for playing both sides of the market would have to-

TABLE 13
Purchases and sales with Predictor 6
(1965–1977).

Purchases	Sales
86.12 (January 1965)	92.69 (February 1966)
80.99 (November 1966)	102.04 (January 1969)
82.58 (September 1970)	90.05 (December 1970)
97.11 (February 1971)	114.62 (February 1973)
92.49 (July 1975)	100.57 (March 1977)
97.75 (August 1977)	91.00 (December 1977)
Long positions: 91 months	Total return: 61.8%
Short positions: 65 months	Total return: 46.8%
Annual return: 8.35% per year	
8.24% per year—long side only	

TABLE 14
Demonstration of buy and sell signals with Predictor 6 (32 months).

Month	Stock Prices	Earnings	Month	Stock Prices	Earnings
Aug. (1968)	98.11	$92.16	Dec.	91.11	$90.61
Sept.	101.34	92.85	Jan. (1970)	90.31	90.00
Oct.	103.76	91.91	Feb.	87.16	89.83
Nov.	105.40	91.00	March	88.65	89.94
Dec.	106.48	91.64	April	85.95	89.11
Jan. (1969)	102.04 SELL	90.67	May	76.06	89.44
Feb.	101.46	90.17	June	75.59	90.35
March	99.30	90.31	July	75.52	90.99
April	101.26	90.22	Aug.	77.92	91.34
May	104.62	91.00	Sept.	82.58 BUY	90.55
June	99.14	91.31	Oct.	84.37	89.63
July	94.71	91.37	Nov.	84.28	90.35
Aug.	94.18	91.44	Dec.	90.05 SELL	90.81
Sept.	94.51	92.17	Jan. (1971)	93.49	91.68
Oct.	95.52	91.20	Feb.	97.11 BUY	92.06
Nov.	96.21	90.53	March	99.60	92.14

taled 109 percent, or 8.35 percent per year. The player who confined his transactions to the long side of the market would have averaged an 8.24 percent annual return on his investment.

As in the case of the predictors presented earlier, I think it is important to demonstrate Predictor 6 with real data for stock prices and spendable earnings, corrected for inflation. Table 14 provides such a demonstration for 32 months. The table begins in August 1968, with the S&P 500 at 98.11, weekly earnings at $92.16, and a buy signal that has already been in force for nearly two years. September earnings increased to $92.85, so we held our long position. However, October earnings declined to $91.91, a loss of 94¢. Since the loss of 94¢ was less than $1.00, we held our positions and waited for the November earnings. These were $91.00, a loss of 91¢ from October. Since any two consecutive monthly losses of more than 40¢ each define a sell signal, the November earnings were the signal to sell out of the 1967–1968 bull market. Because earnings are usually reported five to six weeks late, we would have sold in January 1969, with the S&P 500 at 102.04.

Now that a sell signal has been activated, we want to check the months ahead for buy signals. December 1968 earnings were up 64¢, but January 1969 earnings were down 97¢. February was down farther, and March showed a slight increase, followed by a slight decrease in April 1969. Finally, weekly earnings posted a 78¢ gain for May 1969. Following our trading rule, a buy signal will be given if June's earnings can increase by at least 40¢. But the actual increase for June 1969 was only 31¢, so there was no buy signal. The increase for September 1969 was 73¢, but the October increase of 3¢ also failed to meet the 40¢ requirement.

With a sell signal still in force, we see nothing but minor fluctuations in spendable earnings until June 1970, when there was a 91¢ increase from May. July 1970 added a 64¢ increase from June. That's a 91¢ and 64¢ increase for two consecutive months, and the buy signal brought us back into the long side of the market in September 1970, with the S&P 500 at 82.58. August earnings increased, but there was a 79¢ decrease for September 1970, and an additional 92¢ decline in October 1970, so we sold in December at 90.05. Finally, November earnings increased by 72¢ and December earnings were up 46¢, and we bought back into the new bull market at 97.11 in February 1971.

As may be seen from Table 14, Predictor 6 works reasonably well. It sold us out one month after the top of the 1967–1968 bull market, kept us out of a serious market decline of 18 months, and then bought us back in only two months after the July bottom of the 1970 bear market. The indicator then flashed a false sell signal at the beginning of the 1971 bull market, but it reversed itself only two months later. We missed only seven points of the new bull market. True spendable earnings is far from a perfect stock market forecaster, but it has performed well from 1965 through 1977.

Future Prospects for Predictor 6

In my opinion the forecasting accuracy of Predictor 6 will continue into the future. There are several reasons for this expectation, but I will discuss only the two most important reasons here. First, sustained economic prosperity in the United States has always been closely related to the power of labor to purchase the goods it manufactures. Historically, there has been a condition of economic prosperity in the United States for most of the last 100 years, though I will presently describe some important exceptions to this generalization. Second, the problem of sustaining the purchasing power of wages during high inflation has become even more critical in recent years because of the changing inventory policies of large corporations. When faced with the prospect of continuing inflation, large manufacturers, wholesalers, and retailers have sought to build up extremely large inventories of raw materials and finished goods. These inventories may offer some hedge against inflation, but frequently they are floated on large bank loans. Given any sort of credit squeeze, these inventories must be unloaded quickly, and this is when purchasing power of workers' earnings becomes decisive. If the wages have kept pace with inflation, the inventories will be reduced far more quickly than if wages have lagged behind inflation. The economic recession of late 1973, 1974, and early 1975 was worsened by the inability of workers to purchase the inventories that had been stockpiled, and industrial production was severely cut back until these inventories were reduced. However, if wages had kept pace with inflation during this period, both the recession and its impact on the stock market would have been much less severe. These are only a few of the reasons why I think that Predictor 6 will extend its forecasting power into future market cycles.

As always, the alert market player should be on the lookout for future circumstances that may distort the forecasting power of his indicators. In the case of Predictor 6, I want to mention two potential sources of distortion. The first is U.S.

exports abroad. A large increase in U.S. exports of durable consumer goods might sustain high industrial production despite a decline in the purchasing power of workers' earnings. Second, if new technologies of industrial production (for example, automation) should require unexpectedly large initial investments of capital, then real wages might fall despite increased general economic prosperity. In either case, the market forecasting power of Predictor 6 might be distorted.

With respect to the two specific trading rules for real wages, it should be noted that this series contains many minor fluctuations, especially at major turning points in the market. It is essential that the player not try to buy and sell at every minor fluctuation in spendable earnings. This is an intermediate-term indicator that will not work very well if it is misused as a short-term indicator. The few points that are sacrificed by acting a month or two or three after major market tops and bottoms are very little compared to the commissions and losses that will beset the player who tries to buy or sell after each minor fluctuation in Predictor 6. For the player who wants to experiment with his own trading rules for Predictor 6, the necessary data are included in the Appendix.

Recency and Availability of Data for Predictor 6

Monthly data for real spendable earnings are usually reported around the end of the month for the preceding month. For example, May data will be available at the end of June or in early July. Thus, the market player will be acting on information that is about five or six weeks old by the time it arrives. If the player has some way of obtaining earlier information, it would offer some advantage in timing purchases and sales.

Real spendable weekly earnings are published in the *Survey of Current Business*. A closely related series of true hourly wages is published monthly in *Economic Indicators,* but the player should develop his own trading rules if he plans to trade the market with hourly wages. Finally, *Barron's* and *The Wall Street Journal* occasionally publish recent values of real spendable weekly earnings. All these publications are available at large and medium-size libraries, and usually at smaller libraries as well.

Predictor 7: Bankers' Security Loans

The manager at your local bank might be willing to loan you money to buy your favorite stock, but you shouldn't count on it. However, the practices of banking for individual depositors in the suburbs are entirely different from the practices of corporate finance banking. The latter is an immensely complicated business, which involves corporate bankers in dealings with all levels of government, foreign nations, international corporations, underwriting houses, insurance companies, and virtually every other major financial institution in the world. In the course of their business, finance bankers accept stock as loan collateral, they trade stocks for their own accounts, and they sometimes loan money to businesses, nations, and individuals for the purposes of purchasing stock. It is this last function of finance banking, loaning money to purchase or carry securities, that provides Predictor 7.

The amount of money bankers have loaned for carrying securities is an excellent indicator of major money movements to and from stocks a few months later. Like several of our other predictors, bankers' security loans serve as an early indicator of the availability of money for stock in the near future. Increasing bankers' loans are a reliable sign of money ahead for stock, and indicate that the market averages will advance. However, when bankers' loans are declining, the market is approaching a period of tight money and stock prices decline. Figure 9 shows bankers' security loans for the 13 years from 1965 through 1977. First let's take a look at the general relationship between changes in bankers' loans and changes in the stock market average.

FIGURE 9.
Predictor 7: Bankers' security loans 1965–1977 (in billions).

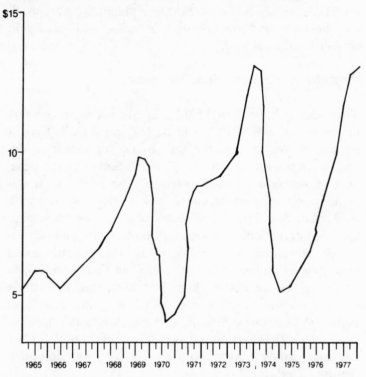

The year of 1965 begins with bankers' security loans at a little over $6 billion and a market that is going into the last year of a major bull swing. Both series increased together through the opening months of 1965, but bankers' loans topped out in June 1965, seven months before the bull market topped out in January 1966. Declining bankers' loans led the short 1966 bear market. When the market finally hit bottom in October 1966, bankers' loans bottomed out one month later at $5.3 billion.

In the next complete market cycle, bankers' loans and the market averages increased together through all of 1967 and most of 1968. However, bankers' loans topped out at $10.2 billion in September 1968, three months before the bull market ended in December 1968. The bear swing for this cycle lasted 19 months, and both stocks and bankers' loans bottomed out in July 1970.

In the 1971–1974 cycle, bankers' loans led the market averages again. In the bull market of 1971–1972, bankers' loans and the market averages rose together. Finally, bankers' loans topped out at $12.5 billion in December 1972. One month later, in January 1973, the S&P 500 reached its all-time high, and the great bull market was over. During the 1973–1974 bear market, the decline in bankers' loans for securities continued to lead the falling market averages. Bankers' loans, however, bottomed out in June 1974, four months before the market bottom of October 1974. Bankers' loans and the market averages increased together through the 1975–1976 bull market. When the last bull market topped out in January 1977, bankers' loans did not top out but fluctuated erratically through the 1977 market decline.

In summary, tops and bottoms of bankers' loans have run ahead of or coincided with five of the seven major turning points in the 1965–1977 stock market. For the sixth turning point, bankers' loans trailed the market by a single month, and they fluctuated following the seventh market turn. Clearly, this is a predictor with at least some forecasting value. Our next concern is to develop the trading rules that yield the greatest profit for playing the market averages with bankers' security loans. Over the past 13 years the following trading rules have returned reasonable profits:

> BUY *when the two most recent months of bankers' security loans exceed the two previous months of loans.*
>
> SELL *(or sell short) when the two most recent months of bankers' security loans are less than the two previous months of loans.*

Table 15 shows the dates of transactions and the profits that would have been made by the trader who played the market with our trading rules from 1965 through 1977. Profits would have averaged 6.9 percent per year for the trader who played both sides of the market, and 7.42 percent per year for playing the long side of the market only.

In order to clarify the use of both trading rules, Table 16 presents a brief forecasting demonstration with recent data for stock market prices and bankers' security loans. Table 16 begins with November 1972. A buy signal was in force, and bankers' security loans for the two most recent months (October and November 1972) totaled $24.086 billion. Loans for the two previous months (August and September 1972) totaled $22.203 billion. Since the loan total for the two most recent months was greater than the loan total for the two previous months, the buy signal was continued into the next month. For December 1972, the loan total for the two most

TABLE 15
Purchases and sales with Predictor 7
(1965–1977).

Purchases	Sales
86.12 (January 1965)	89.38 (September 1965)
93.32 (January 1966)	91.60 (April 1966)
86.06 (June 1966)	77.81 (September 1966)
87.36 (February 1967)	92.59 (May 1967)
95.81 (September 1967)	97.87 (May 1968)
98.11 (August 1968)	102.04 (January 1969)
99.30 (March 1969)	101.26 (April 1969)
94.18 (August 1969)	96.21 (November 1969)
87.16 (February 1970)	85.95 (April 1970)
75.59 (June 1970)	75.72 (July 1970)
84.37 (October 1970)	103.04 (April 1971)
97.24 (August 1971)	110.27 (April 1973)
105.61 (September 1973)	102.03 (November 1973)
69.44 (October 1974)	67.07 (December 1974)
80.10 (February 1975)	99.05 (April 1977)
100.18 (July 1977)	94.28 (November 1977)

Long positions: 97 months	Total return: 59.9%
Short positions: 59 months	Total return: 29.6%

Annual return: 6.90% per year
7.42% per year—long side only

TABLE 16
Demonstration of buy and sell signals with Predictor 7 (26 months).

Month	Stock Prices	Bankers' Loans (in millions)	
		Two Most Recent Months	Two Previous Months
Nov. (1972)	115.05	$24,086	$22,203
Dec.	117.05	24,403	23,497
Jan. (1973)	118.42	24,542	24,086
Feb.	114.62 SELL	23,464	24,403
March	112.42	22,129	24,542
April	110.27	20,726	23,464
May	107.22	20,174	22,129
June	104.75	19,800	20,726
July	105.83 BUY	21,828	20,174
Aug.	103.80	21,768	19,800
Sept.	105.61 SELL	18,941	21,828
Oct.	109.84	18,809	21,768
Nov.	102.03	18,690	18,941
Dec.	94.78	18,615	18,809
Jan. (1974)	96.11	17,528	18,690
Feb.	93.45	17,249	18,615
March	97.44	17,347	17,528
April	92.46	16,610	17,249
May	89.67	16,344	17,347
June	89.79	12,745	16,610
July	82.82	14,030	16,344
Aug.	76.03 BUY	18,000	12,745
Sept.	68.12	16,123	14,030
Oct.	69.44 SELL	14,743	18,000
Nov.	71.74	14,823	16,123
Dec.	67.07 BUY	15,128	14,743

recent months was still greater than the total for the two previous months. The difference also favored recent months over previous months through January 1973.

However, at the end of February, total loans for the two most recent months dropped to $23.464 billion, while the loan total for the two previous months rose to $24.403 billion. This was a sell signal, since recent months' loans had fallen below the previous months' loans. Since bankers' security loans are reported five to six weeks late, we would have actually sold out (or gone short) in early April 1973, with the S&P 500 at 110.27. For March, April, May, and June of 1973, total loans for recent months remained below the loan totals of the two previous months. However, in July 1973, recent months' loans rose to $21.828 billion, higher than the $20.174 billion for the two previous months. This was a buy signal, and we would have covered our short positions and bought back into the market at 105.61 in September 1973. However, the buy signal at the end of July was false, and at the end of September 1973, recent months again dropped below previous months. We would have sold in November 1973 at 102.03, for a loss of about three points in the worst bear market since the 1930s.

Through the rest of 1973 and early 1974, the bear market started to fall apart, and bankers' loans moved right in step with the decline. Month after month the total of recent bankers' loans remained below the total of previous bankers' loans. Finally, at the end of August 1974, recent months' loans surpassed previous months' loans, and a buy signal was given. We bought into the market in October 1974, with the S&P 500 at 69.44. Although recent months' loans for September remained ahead of previous months, there was another sell signal at the end of October, so we sold in December at 67.07. Finally, the December loan figures indicate the last buy signal in our demonstration. At the end of December 1974, recent bankers' loans drew ahead of previous loans, and we bought into the market in February 1975, the second month of the 1975–1976 bull swing.

The most important conclusion that follows from our demonstration is that predictor 7 works more often than it fails. We lost six points in a market slide of 51 points, and those who went short on the sell signals would have cleaned up in the 1973–1974 bear market. While you probably cannot take a serious loss on the market averages with Predictor 7, you may sacrifice a few points here and there on false signals.

Future Prospects for Predictor 7

It is my opinion that bankers' security loans will forecast future market changes as accurately as they predicted the market averages from 1965 through 1977. The amount of money bankers have loaned for carrying securities is a leading indicator of the much larger amounts of money that will be moving into or out of stocks a few months ahead. It is important to remember, however, that this relationship is merely correlational rather than causal. Changes of a billion dollars or two in bankers' security loans correspond to changes of hundreds of billions of dollars in stock values during major market swings. Hence, the predictive value of bankers' loans may be susceptible to distortion.

The alert market player will attend to any developments that might distort the forecasting power of Predictor 7 in the future. Here are a couple of possibilities. First, the amounts of money that finance bankers are permitted to loan for security purchases are presently limited by law. Changing legal restrictions on bankers' security loans might distort the accuracy of Predictor 7. A second recent change in the practice of finance banking might also have implications for the accuracy of Predictor 7. This is the rapidly increasing participation of banks in the stock market as brokers and traders for their own accounts and the accounts of their customers. In the last decade, banks have enjoyed much faster growth in their securities transactions than in their other services. It's difficult to state exactly what this means for the future of Predictor 7, but here are two possibilities. If banks continue to prosper in their securities transactions, then bankers' security loans may increase sharply in the years ahead. But if several major banks are seriously burned in their securities transactions, then bankers' loans for securities may drop off sharply. Either outcome could distort the forecasting power of Predictor 7.

Finally, I want to state as clearly as possible that Predictor 7 works because it anticipates major movements of money to and from stocks in the near future. It does not work because finance bankers are geniuses at market forecasting who adjust their security loans accordingly. Nothing could be farther from the truth. The average finance banker has a record of market forecasting that is probably a little worse than the forecasting record of the average Wall Street professional—in other words, *terrible*. In the 1973–1974 bear market, several of our largest and most respected banks took a real bath. The lesson cannot be repeated too often: your banker is no more capable of forecasting the next major market swing than your stockbroker, dentist, barber, or father-in-law. What other people say about the market should be ignored; only what the predictors say should be heeded.

The specific trading rules for Predictor 7 present more of a problem than the trading rules for our other predictors. Part of the reason for this is that while bankers' security loans are reasonably good indicators of bull market tops and bear market bottoms, this series shows some problems in forecasting intermediate market changes. The problem is greatest during the first swing of bull markets and during the final months of bear markets. At both periods the market may rise or fall considerably while Predictor 7 gives a series of inconsistent signals. One solution to this problem is simply to ignore Predictor 7 when it forecasts erratically and to use the ten remaining predictors. A second solution is to eliminate some of the inconsistency by developing new trading rules that ignore the smaller changes in bankers' security loans. An example of the second solution would be the use of longer monthly moving averages to smooth out the series. As a case in point, I have had some success redefining buy and sell signals in terms of more complicated trading rules that I have not presented here because so many market players are allergic to more than simple arithmetic. Readers who are not so allergic might want to develop their own trading rules for Predictor 7, an effort for which the necessary data have been included in the Appendix.

Recency and Availability of Data for Predictor 7

Bankers' security loans are reported five to six weeks late. The player who uses Predictor 7 will be acting about six or seven weeks after the end of the month for which the data are reported. I don't know of any way to obtain earlier information for Predictor 7, but if the player could obtain such information, it would probably improve the timing of his transactions to a worthwhile extent.

Data for bankers' security loans are reported monthly in the *Survey of Current Business*. This publication is available at most libraries. The series is occasionally shown in the leading financial periodicals, such as *The Wall Street Journal* and *Barron's*, but not frequently enough to rely on.

Predictor 8: Brokers' Margin Credit

Predictor 8 is the first cousin of Predictor 7. Just as bankers loan money for carrying securities, all major brokerage firms also have provisions to lend money for others to buy stock. The only important difference between the two situations is that the brokers are more likely than bankers to loan smaller amounts to a greater number of clients. A second difference is that borrowings from the banks are called loans, whereas borrowings from a brokerage firm are called margin credit.

The total margin credit brokers have extended to their clients turns out to be an excellent forecaster of changing market averages in the months ahead. As might be expected, when total margin credit increases, the market averages rise, while declining margin credit forecasts lower stock prices in the coming months. Again we seem to have an indicator that gives an early signal about future movements of larger sums of money to and from stocks.

Figure 10 presents a more detailed picture of the relationship between margin credit and the stock market averages between 1965 and 1978. So let's take a closer look at Predictor 8. The figure begins in 1965. Margin credit was

FIGURE 10.
Predictor 8: Brokers' margin credit 1965–1977 (in billions).

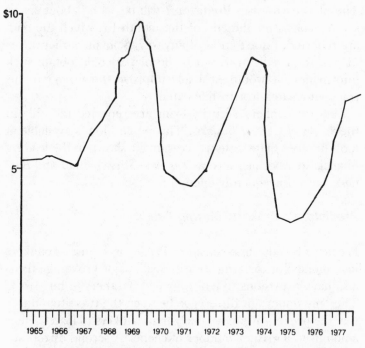

approximately $5 billion, and the market was entering the last year of a major bull swing. Total margin credit advanced to $5.5 billion by the end of 1965. The bull market topped out in January 1966, but margin credit continued upward until it topped out at $5.8 billion, three months behnd the market. However, margin credit quickly caught up with the short 1966 bear market. Stock prices and margin credit both bottomed out together in October 1966.

The next complete market cycle included the bull market of 1967–1968. Market averages and margin credit both rose together for 26 months. The market finally topped out at 106.48 in December 1968, and margin credit topped out at slightly less than $10 billion the same month. During the bear market phase of this cycle, stock prices and margin credit fell together through all of 1969 and well into 1970.

Margin credit finally bottomed out at $5 billion in July 1970, the last month of the bear market.

Our third complete cycle begins with the bull market of 1971–1972. Margin credit and stock prices rose through the second half of 1970 and all of 1971 and 1972. In December 1972, margin credit topped out at $8 billion. One month later, in January 1973, the bull market peaked and turned downward. Declining margin credit led declining stock prices through the entire bear market fiasco of 1973–1974. When margin credit bottomed out in December 1974, at less than $4 billion, the recovery in stock prices was not far off. As if on cue, January 1975 kicked off the next bull market. The two series rose together once again through the last bull market of 1975–1976. However, brokers' margin credit increased slightly after the January 1977 market top.

In general, Predictor 8 has compiled a reasonable forecasting record for the 13 years under study. Although total margin credit missed the short 1966 market break by three months, it has coincided with or led every other major market turn except the last one. Our next concern is to develop the most profitable trading rules for playing the market averages with margin credit. Not surprisingly, the same two trading rules that were developed for bankers' security loans also work fairly well for brokers' margin credit:

> BUY *when the two most recent months of margin credit are greater than the two previous months of margin credit.*
>
> SELL *(or sell short) when the two most recent months of margin credit are less than the two previous months of margin credit.*

Table 17 shows that the player who traded both sides of the 1965–1977 market with our trading rules would have averaged profits of 7.2 percent per year. Annual profits would have averaged 6.43 percent for the player who traded the long side of the market only. Both figures represent rates of return that are satisfactory but hardly outstanding.

TABLE 17
Purchases and sales with Predictor 8
(1965–1977).

Purchases	Sales
86.12 (January 1965)	86.49 (August 1965)
92.15 (November 1965)	85.84 (July 1966)
84.45 (January 1967)	95.67 (April 1968)
100.53 (June 1968)	103.76 (October 1968)
105.40 (November 1968)	99.30 (March 1969)
94.71 (July 1969)	94.18 (August 1969)
90.31 (January 1970)	87.16 (February 1970)
75.72 (July 1970)	114.62 (February 1973)
92.46 (April 1974)	89.79 (June 1974)
83.78 (March 1975)	91.00 (December 1977)

Long positions:	107 months	Total return: 57.3%
Short positions:	49 months	Total return: 36.3%

Annual return:	7.20% per year	
	6.43% per year—long side only	

Table 18 presents a 30-month demonstration of our trading rules for real market prices and margin credits. The
table begins at September 1972. A buy signal was in force,
and the total margin credit for the two most recent months
(August and September) was \$16.143 billion. The total
margin credit for the two previous months (June and July
1972) was \$15.737 billion. Since the total margin for recent
months was greater than the total for previous months, the
buy signal was continued and we held our long position.

Recent months' margin continued ahead of the previous
months' total through October, November, and December
1972. But at the end of January 1973, recent months'
margin fell below the margin total for previous months. This
provided a sell signal, and since data on margin credit report
only two to three weeks late, the player would have sold the
S&P 500 at 114.62 in February 1973.

At this point the 1973–1974 bear market started to gather
momentum. From February to the end of 1973, stock prices
dropped nearly 20 points. And for each remaining month of

1973, the total for recent months' margin was less than the total for previous months' margin. This trend continued through the first two months of the next year, but in March 1974, recent months' margin finally pulled ahead of previous months, and we bought into the market at 92.46 in

TABLE 18
Demonstration of buy and sell signals with Predictor 8 (30 months).

Month	Stock Prices	Margin Credit	
		Two Most Recent Months (in millions)	Two Previous Months (in millions)
Sept. (1972)	109.39	$16,143	$15,737
Oct.	109.56	16,164	16,005
Nov.	115.05	16,247	16,143
Dec.	117.50	16,346	16,164
Jan. (1973)	118.42 SELL	16,155	16,247
Feb.	114.62	15,748	16,346
March	112.42	15,241	16,155
April	110.27	14,781	15,748
May	107.22	14,077	15,241
June	104.75	13,200	14,761
July	105.83	12,657	14,077
August	103.80	12,299	13,200
Sept.	105.61	12,005	12,657
Oct.	109.84	11,861	12,299
Nov.	102.03	11,583	12,005
Dec.	94.78	10,922	11,861
Jan. (1974)	96.11	10,574	11,583
Feb.	93.45	10,746	10,922
March	97.44 BUY	10,942	10,574
April	92.46	11,077	10,746
May	89.67 SELL	10,919	10,942
June	89.79	10,621	11,077
July	82.82	10,185	10,919
August	76.03	9,597	10,621
Sept.	68.12	8,845	10,185
Oct.	69.44	8,253	9,597
Nov.	71.74	8,183	8,845
Dec.	67.07	8,083	8,253
Jan. (1975)	72.56	8,066	8,183
Feb.	80.10 BUY	8,355	8,083

April 1974. However, in May, only two months later, another sell signal was given, and we sold out at 89.79, in June 1974, losing less than three points on the false buy signal. The bear market wasn't over yet. Finally, the market bottomed out in December 1974. The recent months' margin bottomed out in January 1975, and it drew ahead of the previous month's total in February. In March, we bought into the third month of the 1975–1976 bull market.

I regard Table 18 as an excellent demonstration of the forecasting power of Predictor 8. It sold us out just one month after the top of the greatest bull market in history. It held our losses to three points in the worst bear market since 1938, a bear market that lost a total of 51 points. Predictor 8 then bought us back into the market only two months after the 1975–1976 bull swing began. Margin credit will not always provide such accurate forecasting, but it's usually accurate enough to keep you ahead of the game.

Future Prospects for Predictor 8

It is probable that Predictor 8 will continue its forecasting accuracy into future market cycles. Brokers' margin credit forecasts successfully because the indicator is sensitive to the earliest changes in the supply and demand for money, changes that will be reflected in stock market prices a few months later. I do not foresee any probable circumstances that will alter the sensitivity of Predictor 8 and distort its forecasting power, and I have more confidence in the future of brokers' margin credit than bankers' loans as a predictor of future stock prices. One reason for this evaluation is that Predictor 8 has already done a slightly better job of forecasting the 1965–1977 market changes than Predictor 7.

A second reason for optimism about the forecasting future of brokers' margin credit is that it's difficult to envision circumstances (economic or otherwise) that would be likely to distort the predictor. For example, margin requirements for purchasing stock have been at 50 percent now for several years. If the stock exchange were to suddenly change its margin requirements, the overall total of brokers' margin credit might suddenly increase or decrease, but the forecasting power of the new series would probably continue much as before.

In assessing the future prospects of Predictor 8, the alert player might want to beware of events that decrease the demand for margin during bull markets and increase the supply of margin during bear markets. For reasons that are not yet clear, margin credit advanced slightly during the 1977 bear market, but I believe that Predictor 8 will quickly resume its forecasting power. You have already learned that no indicator forecasts perfectly. The second great truth of market forecasting is that no indicator forecasts forever. One day, though nobody can say when, there will be a market cycle that cannot be forecast with any of our indicators. In my judgment, however, that day is a long way off.

The specific trading rules for Predictor 8 seem to work reasonably well, but I encourage all alert market players to develop their own trading rules for margin credit (the necessary data are in the Appendix). In particular, the trader should explore the possibility of developing asymmetrical trading rules that require margin credit to advance at a specific rate to maintain purchasing signals. Brokers' margin credit has been useful for market forecasting because the series shows large numbers of consecutive runs and very few reversals, hence all reversals at least raise the possibility of a major turn in the market. Since our trading rules are probably more likely to be late at bull market tops than at bear market bottoms, players who plan to develop their own trading rules should devote their initial efforts to defining different buy signals.

Recency and Availability of Data for Predictor 8

Data for brokers' margin credit are published in *Barron's*, a weekly which is available at most libraries. The figures are typically two to three weeks late, allowing the player to act before the end of the month following the month for which the data are reported. This series also appears in the *Survey of Current Business,* but it is too many months in arrears to allow profitable trading. Finally, the information for Predictor 8 can also be obtained directly from the New York Stock Exchange.

Predictor 9: The Price of Gold

Although modern currencies are no longer backed by precious metals, many investors and speculators continue to be fascinated by the financial chimera of owning or trading gold. It is little short of amazing that gold still commands a following, because the reasons most often given for investment in gold are simply wrong. Ownership of gold, it is argued (by some who should know better), protects the investor from instability in the purchasing power of his currency, and especially from the ravages of inflation. As applied to the United States, this is utter nonsense, and two examples should suffice to eliminate this sort of twaddle. Our first example is from more than 100 years ago. During a financial panic in the 1870s, gold sold for $168 an ounce. Recently gold sold for $800 an ounce. If a person or family had invested in gold a hundred years ago, the purchasing power of their investment would have declined by over 90 percent. In 1870, $168 would have easily purchased more than four times the goods and services that $800 will purchase today. How about a second example? At the bottom of the Great Depression of the 1930s, the United States fixed the price of gold at $35 per ounce. So in the last 45 years the price of gold has increased about 20-fold, while the purchasing power of the dollar is about a ninth of its 1932 value. That's not much of a hedge against inflation. Finally, consider the person or family who purchased gold at $168 in 1870 and sold gold at $35 per ounce in 1932. That's a loss of about 80 percent on a 60-year investment.

The truth about "investing" in gold is simple. You cannot invest in gold; you can only speculate in gold. If you want to speculate in gold, I wish you every success, but you shouldn't confuse speculation with investment. Historically, the purchasing power of gold has been far more variable and much less predictable than the purchasing power of the dollar. Keep this in mind the next time someone tries to sell you gold as an "investment." You'll be far better off with a straight 5 percent savings account or a U.S. Savings Bond.

Having learned this much about the history of gold prices, you should also know that there is a fairly reliable relationship between gold and stock prices: they usually move in opposite directions. During major financial crises, the loss of confidence in the economy is reflected by an increased demand for gold. As the crisis deepens, more and more money moves away from stock and into gold. When the price of gold finally tops out, the lack of confidence in the economy has passed, the bear market bottoms out, and stock prices move into the first stage of the next bull market.

The opposite story unfolds during major bull markets. As economic prosperity and confidence in the market increase, fewer investors want gold at its previous prices. The demand falls month after month, and gold is often selling at new lows by the time the bull market tops out and the bear market begins.

Can we use the price of gold as an indicator for forecasting stock market averages? The answer is yes, but only when gold is traded freely. From the 1930s through the early 1970s, gold prices were fixed by international financial agreements that were supported by all major Western powers. Since 1972, however, gold has once again been traded on open markets.

Figure 11 shows the price of gold between 1972 and 1978. Let's compare these six years of gold prices with the stock market averages for the same period. At the start of 1972, gold was selling for $43 an ounce, and stocks were entering the last year of the 1971–1972 bull market. In the first six months of the year, gold rose to $70 and then dropped back to approximately $64 at the end of 1972.

FIGURE 11.
Predictor 9: Gold prices 1972–1977.

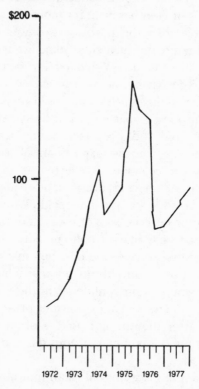

The bull market topped out in January 1973, and gold prices rose from $64 to $127 in less than six months. A second retreat to $91 occurred in late 1973, but gold was selling for $117 an ounce at the end of 1973. In the first few months of 1974, gold soared to $180. It then backed off to $140 in mid-1974, and the bear market took a breather. However, when gold advanced again in July 1974, it was a reliable indicator that the bear market still had a way to go. In December of 1974 gold finally topped out at $195 an ounce, and the bear market in stocks bottomed out the same month.

Through 1975, gold prices retreated from $195 to $145

during the first year of the new bull market. Gold prices drifted slightly lower in 1976, the second year of the bull market. Gold finally bottomed out in November 1976, and the bull market topped out two months later. Gold prices then advanced sharply through the 1977 market decline. It is apparent that gold prices and the stock market averages move in opposite directions, and our next task is to develop trading rules that exploit this relationship for maximum forecasting profitability.

Here are two trading rules for playing the market with the price of gold:

> BUY *when the prices of gold for the two most recent months are less than the prices of gold for the two previous months.*
>
> SELL (*or sell short*) *when the prices of gold for the two most recent months are greater than the prices of gold for the two previous months.*

In Table 19 we can see the profits generated by following these two trading rules for the 1972–1977 market averages. Profits averaged 12.4 percent per year for the trader who played both sides of the market and 10.4 percent per year

TABLE 19
Purchases and sales with Predictor 9
(1972–1977).

Purchases	Sales
108.11 (June 1972)	111.01 (August 1972)
109.56 (October 1972)	114.62 (February 1973)
105.61 (September 1973)	102.03 (November 1973)
68.12 (September 1974)	71.74 (November 1974)
80.10 (February 1975)	100.96 (February 1977)
99.29 (June 1977)	96.23 (September 1977)
Long positions: 37 months	Total return: 32.2%
Short positions: 30 months	Total return: 37.2%
Annual return: 12.4% per year	
10.4% per year—long side only	

for those who played the long side of the market only. Both are excellent rates of return on capital investment.

Table 20 provides a short demonstration of both trading rules with real data for gold prices and stock prices. The

TABLE 20
Demonstration of buy and sell signals with Predictor 9 (33 months).

| | | Gold Prices | |
| | | | |
Month	Stock Prices	Two Most Recent Months	Two Previous Months
June (1972)	108.01 BUY	$128	$137
July	107.21	$130	$132
August	111.01 SELL	$135	$128
Sept.	109.39	$136	$130
Oct.	109.56 BUY	$133	$135
Nov.	115.05	$128	$136
Dec.	117.50	$125	$133
Jan. (1973)	118.42	$127	$128
Feb.	114.62 SELL	$133	$125
March	112.42	$147	$127
April	110.27	$160	$133
May	107.22	$171	$147
June	104.75	$190	$160
July	105.83	$216	$171
August	103.80	$221	$190
Sept.	105.61 BUY	$208	$216
Oct.	109.84	$203	$221
Nov.	102.03 SELL	$209	$208
Dec.	94.78	$211	$203
Jan. (1974)	96.11	$231	$209
Feb.	93.45	$270	$211
March	97.44	$302	$231
April	92.46	$329	$270
May	89.67	$333	$302
June	89.79	$331	$329
July	82.82	$336	$333
August	76.03	$341	$331
Sept.	68.12 BUY	$329	$336
Oct.	69.44	$315	$341
Nov.	71.74 SELL	$333	$329
Dec.	67.07	$365	$315
Jan. (1975)	72.56	$366	$333
Feb.	80.10 BUY	$353	$365

demonstration begins with June 1972, and the prices for gold for the two most recent months total to less than the price total for the two previous months. This defines a buy signal, so we bought into the market with the S&P 500 at 108.01. Recent months' totals remained below previous months' totals through August 1972, but in August the two recent months' total ($135) increased over the two previous months ($128), and we sold out of the market at 111.01. Recent months continued ahead of previous months through September, but previous months drew ahead of recent months in October 1972, and we bought back in at 109.56.

The October 1972 buy signal remained in force through the rest of 1972 and January 1973, the month of the 1971–1972 bull market top. One month later, in February 1973, total gold prices for the two most recent months moved ahead of prices for the two previous months, and we sold the S&P 500 at 114.62. As the 1973 bear market gathered momentum, prices for recent months' gold continued their lead over previous months. Finally, in September 1973, recent months' gold fell below previous months ($208 vs. $216), and we bought into the market at 105.61. However, this false buy signal lasted only through October. The predictor corrected itself in November 1973, and we sold at 102.03, taking a four-point loss in a bear market that eventually lost 51 points.

Through each declining month of the 1974 bear market, gold prices for the two most recent months remained ahead of gold prices for the two previous months. When recent months' prices finally dropped below previous months' prices in September 1974, the bear market was over. We bought into the market with the S&P 500 at 68.12, made about three points before the false sell signal in November at 71.74, and then bought into the second month of the last bull market in February 1975. Predictor 9 missed the bull market top by one month and the bear market bottom by two months. It will not always be quite so accurate in future market cycles, but it will usually catch the major market swings.

Future Prospects for Predictor 9

Gold prices and stock prices have a long and consistent history of moving in opposite directions, and they will probably continue to do so in future market cycles. However, the alert market player should always remember that the relationship is quite general. Predictor 9 forecasts quite accurately for the major market swings and reasonably well for intermediate changes in the market averages. But gold prices are not useful for short-term market forecasting, and they should not be used for this purpose.

The human psychology that underlies Predictor 9 provides further evidence for its continuity as a forecaster of future market cycles. When business conditions are poor and stocks are declining, many investors, speculators, and institutions want to channel their money into investments that look safe. For some people, gold appears to meet this requirement. The more serious the loss of confidence in the economy, the better gold looks by comparison, and as the market slide continues, speculators will eventually run the price of gold up to incredible levels. However, even the most enthusiastic gold bugs will eventually realize that the gold has been overbought, and the gold market will start to fall apart. Not coincidentally, the market for stocks bottoms out about the same time, and now the money rushes from gold to stocks, rather than vice versa. It is unlikely that these attitudes will change in future stock market cycles.

The general relationship between gold prices and stock prices will probably continue into future market cycles, but this outcome does not guarantee that our specific trading rules will always provide the most profitable trading strategies. It is my impression that high gold prices are somewhat more accurate predictors of bear market bottoms than low gold prices are predictors of bull market tops. Therefore, the player who wants to use his own trading rules should devote his first efforts to developing different selling signals. The necessary data are included in the Appendix.

Recency and Availability of Data for Predictor 9

Gold prices are published daily in *The Wall Street Journal* and in the financial sections of many metropolitan newspapers. Data are always current, and records are easily maintained. If the player is using monthly closing prices of gold as his data, I recommend acting before the end of the month whenever a new transaction is indicated from the present price trend. Gold prices are extraordinarily volatile, and major price trends can gather tremendous momentum. Whenever it becomes clear which way gold is moving, there is no reason to wait until the end of the month before buying or selling the market.

The market player who wants to speculate directly in gold will find that buying and selling gold futures is more convenient than buying and selling physical quantities of gold. Gold futures are traded on several commodity exchanges. The standard contract is 100 ounces; a single point corresponds to a price change of 10¢ an ounce, for a profit or loss of $10 per point for each contract. Margin requirements are around $1,000 per contract. Gold futures trade in a volatile market, and enormous profits can be won by speculators who can accurately forecast changes in gold prices. Losses will be equally large for speculators who fail in their forecasting.

Predictor 10: Ratio of Corporate Bond Interest Rate to Prime Rate

Long-term and short-term supplies and demands for money often differ from each other, and the difference between long- and short-term interest rates turns out to be a reasonably accurate forecaster of future market averages. The differences in rates, of course, may lie in one of two directions: long-term rates may be higher than short-term rates, or short-term rates may be higher than long-term rates. Let's see how each type of difference affects future stock market prices.

When long-term rates are higher than short-term rates, the immediate demand for loans is being met. Money is relatively loose, and stock prices will rise in the near term. But when short-term rates are higher than long-term interest rates, immediate money is scarcer relative to demand, and stock prices will decline.

If market forecasting with the differences between long- and short-term interest rates is to be profitable, we must next decide which interest rates to compare for the long-term vs. short-term basis. There are three obvious possibilities: government, corporate, and individual borrowing rates. Not surprisingly, the best predictor of changing market prices is the difference in the long- and short-term rates for corporate borrowing. Figure 12 shows the yield on grade Aaa corporate bonds and the prime interest rate for 1965 through 1977. Let's compare the two series in terms of what we already know about the market averages from 1965 through 1977.

First, we can see that corporate bond interest was higher than the prime rate through all of 1965. However, in early 1966, just as the bull market topped out, the prime rate increased over the bond rate. The bear swing of 1966 bottomed out in October, and the prime rate decreased below the bond rate in early 1967. Through the 1967–1968 bull market, the prime rate remained below the bond yield. When the 1968 bull market topped out in December, the prime rate surpassed bond yields a few months later and stayed that way until the bear swing bottomed out in July 1970. Through the bull market of 1971–1972, the prime rate once again yielded less than bonds, and when the greatest bull market in history topped out in January 1973, the prime rate passed the bond rate a few months later. Except for one month in early 1974 the prime rate remained higher than bond yields until the bear market of 1972–1974 bot-

FIGURE 12.
Predictor 10: Aaa bond yields and prime interest rates 1965–1977.

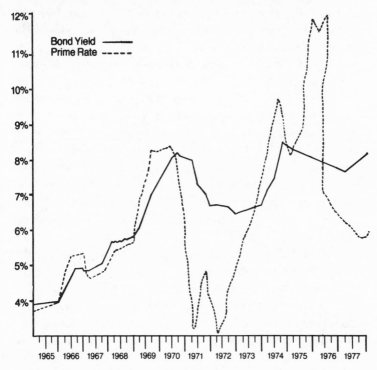

tomed out. Finally, in the last bull market (1975–1976) the prime rate remained below bond yields, but it also remained below bond yields through the 1977 bear market.

In summary, when the prime interest rate is less than the yield from Aaa corporate bonds, the stock market usually goes up, and when the prime rate yields more than bonds, the market goes down. It's that simple, and here are the specific trading rules for Predictor 10:

> BUY *when the prime interest rate is lower than the yield from Aaa corporate bonds.*
>
> SELL (*or sell short*) *when the prime interest rate is higher than the yield from Aaa corporate bonds.*

Table 21 shows the dates of the transactions and the profits that would have resulted from following these trading rules. Returns for 13 years (1965–1977) were 144 percent, or 11.12 percent per year, for playing both sides of the market. Annual profits were 9.31 percent for playing the long side of the market only. Both figures represent substantial investment returns for a 13-year period.

Although Figure 12 has shown the bond yield and prime rate for all 13 years under study, I think it is important to demonstrate both trading rules with real data. Table 22 presents the S&P 500, the Aaa corporate bond yield, and the prime interest rate for 24 months. We begin with May 1973, and the last buy signal is still in force, May bonds yielded 7.29 percent, the prime rate was a slightly lower 7.27 percent, hence the buy signal was unchanged. The yield on June's bonds advanced to 7.37 percent, but the prime rate climbed to 7.99 percent. A sell signal is given whenever the prime rate exceeds bond yields, so we would have sold out of the market (and gone short) in June at 104.75.

Notice that the prime rate remained ahead of bond yields through the rest of 1973 and for January 1974. But in February the prime rate dropped below bond yields, and we

TABLE 21
Purchases and sales with Predictor 10
(1965–1977).

Purchases	Sales
86.12 (January 1965)	93.32 (January 1966)
89.42 (March 1967)	101.26 (April 1969)
75.59 (June 1970)	104.75 (June 1973)
93.45 (February 1974)	97.44 (March 1974)
71.74 (November 1974)	67.07 (December 1974)
72.56 (January 1975)	91.00 (December 1977)

Long positions: 111 months	Total return: 86.1%
Short positions: 45 months	Total return: 58.5%

Annual return: 11.12% per year
9.31% per year—long side only

TABLE 22
Demonstration of buy and sell signals
with Predictor 10 (24 months).

Month	Stock Prices	Bond Yield	Prime Rate
May (1973)	107.22	7.29%	7.27%
June	104.75 SELL	7.37	7.99
July	105.83	7.45	9.18
August	103.80	7.68	10.21
Sept.	105.61	7.63	10.23
Oct.	109.84	7.60	8.92
Nov.	102.03	7.67	8.94
Dec.	94.78	7.68	8.47
Jan. (1974)	96.11	7.83	8.66
Feb.	93.45 BUY	7.85	7.83
March	97.44 SELL	8.01	8.42
April	92.46	8.25	9.79
May	89.67	8.37	10.62
June	89.79	8.47	10.96
July	82.82	8.72	11.72
August	76.03	9.00	11.65
Sept.	68.18	9.24	11.23
Oct.	69.44	9.27	9.36
Nov.	71.74 BUY	8.90	8.81
Dec.	67.07 SELL	8.89	8.98
Jan. (1975)	72.56 BUY	8.83	7.30
Feb.	80.10	8.62	6.33
March	83.78	8.67	6.06
April	84.72	8.95	6.15

bought back in at 93.45. The next month (March 1974), the prime rate once again surpassed bond yields. We sold at 97.44, for a small profit of 3.99 points.

The March 1974 sell signal remained in force through October 1974. In November the prime rate finally dropped below bonds, so we bought at 71.74. The next month (December 1974) found the prime rate at 8.98 percent vs. 8.89 percent for bonds, so we sold for a minor loss of 4.67 points. Finally, in January 1975, the prime rate dropped below the bond yield for good, and we bought at 72.56 to catch the first month of the 1975–1976 bull market.

Predictor 10 gave only two false buy signals through the

worst bear market since 1937–1938, and each signal was corrected the following month. Since we lost four points on one trade and made about four points on the other, we came out about even through the bear market. Short sellers, of course, would have made enormous profits using Predictor 10 through the 1973–1974 bear market.

Future Prospects for Predictor 10

The bond/prime ratio has been a reasonably accurate forecaster of the market, and I think Predictor 10 will hold its forecasting power for many years to come. Large changes in the prime interest are excellent indicators of the supply and demand for short-term (4–6 months) loans. Sharp increases in the prime rate occur simply because money is not available for short-term loans to business. And if loan money is tight for the nation's largest and most powerful corporations, which are the best credit risks in the world, then money isn't going to be available to purchase stocks either. Instead, money will flow out of the market, and stock prices will decline for the intermediate term. Exactly the opposite situation prevails when the prime interest rate moves downward. When short-term loan money is in adequate supply, some of the extra funds will find their way into the market. So will a lot of additional loose money in the general economy, and stock prices will advance.

With respect to our two specific trading rules, the alert market player should keep some of the following contingencies in mind. First, the short-term prime rate is considerably more volatile than the long-term bond yield. Second, this volatility is far greater when the prime rate moves down than when it moves up. Figure 12 shows that the prime rate can follow just behind bond yields for as long as a year in a maturing bull market. Therefore, the bear swing may be well under way before the prime rate actually moves ahead of bond yields. In bull markets, then, it is probably better to risk selling too soon rather than selling too late, and a slightly different trading rule for selling may do better in the future.

This problem doesn't seem to affect bear markets. By the time a bear market has truly bottomed out and the first swing of the next bull market is under way, the prime rate has fallen sharply for several months. If the prime rate has not already fallen below bond yields, it will do so within a couple of months. For the player who wants to devise his own trading rules for Predictor 10, I have included 156 months of prime interest rates and bond yields in the Appendix.

Recency and Availability of Data for Predictor 10

Published values are always recent for the Aaa corporate bond yields and for the prime interest rate. *The Wall Street Journal, Barron's,* and other financial papers periodically publish current values for both series. Changes in the prime interest rate are covered regularly by all but the most backward daily newspapers, and the Sunday financial sections of many papers report both rates on a weekly basis. The information can also be obtained from two federal publications (*Economic Indicators* and *Survey of Current Business*), but the values are four to six weeks old when they are published. Since the market player needs up-to-date information (especially during bull markets), I do not recommend using these federal publications. If all else fails, a phone call to any major brokerage firm or to the investment department of any reasonably large bank will provide current Aaa bond yields and prime interest rates.

Predictor 11: The U.S. Federal Deficit

The professionals of Wall Street must have been looking out the window when Predictor 11 came by. Our last predictor of the stock market averages results from a practice subject to so much economic and moral controversy in its own right that hardly anyone has asked whether changes in federal deficit spending can forecast changes in stock prices. Some financial authorities approve of federal deficit spending, while others believe that it is immoral and dangerous to our economy. But the winning market player keeps his eye on the indicators and leaves the emotional arguments to the losers. The only effect of deficit spending that is important for our purposes is its power to predict stock market prices.

The quarterly deficit of the United States, of course, results from the difference between federal income and federal spending. In theory, the government can lower its deficit by reducing spending or by increasing taxation, and vice versa for increasing the deficit. As a practical matter, however, changes in the deficit are more likely to result from the more sudden changes in tax revenues rather than the slower changes in spending. The last link in this chain of events is provided by the fact that abrupt changes in tax revenues directly affect the money available to the individuals and institutions most likely to buy and sell stock in the near future.

The picture is now complete, albeit greatly oversimplified. A larger deficit generally means lower taxation of the money available to purchase stocks in the near future. In other words, higher deficits lead to higher stock market averages. A smaller deficit entails heavier taxation of funds that would otherwise go into stocks, and the market averages decline.

In Figure 13 we can take a closer look at the relationship between the quarterly federal deficit and the market averages from 1965 through 1977. Figure 13 begins with 1965. The market was entering the last year of a major bull swing, and federal accounts showed a small surplus for the first two quarters of the year. The market advance continued into the second half of 1965, and small deficits were reported for the last two quarters of the year. The bull market topped out in January 1966, the same quarter that federal accounts returned to a surplus. The short 1966 market

FIGURE 13.
Predictor 11: Federal quarterly accounts 1965–1977 (in billions).

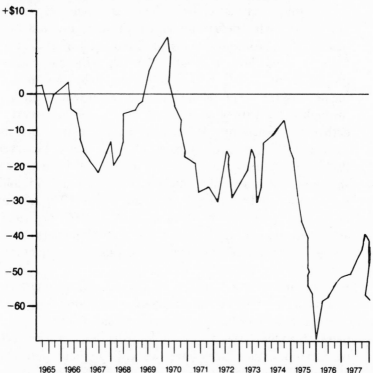

break bottomed out in October, and federal accounts were recording a deficit by the end of September 1966.

In the second complete market cycle, the bull market of 1967–1968 was led by an increased federal deficit for the last quarter of 1966, a very large increase in the deficit for all four quarters of 1967, and large deficits for the first two quarters of 1968. However, the deficit declined sharply in the third and fourth quarters of 1968, and the bull market topped out in December 1968. The 1969–1970 bear market lasted 18 months, and federal accounts showed large surpluses for all four quarters of 1969. The switch back to a deficit in the first quarter of 1970 predicted the end of the bear market. In fact, the second-quarter deficit soared to over $14 billion, and the market bottomed out in July 1970.

Our third market cycle includes the bull market of 1971–1972. The deficit increased through the last two quarters of 1970, remained large through all of 1971, and then retreated slowly through 1972. When the bull market topped out in January 1973, the quarterly deficit was shrinking to less than $11 billion. The deficit declined further through the last three quarters of 1973 as the bear market gathered momentum. Deficits were also extraordinarily small for the first three quarters of 1974, and the market decline continued. Finally, the federal deficit increased sharply to about $25 billion in the last quarter of 1974, and the bear market bottomed out the same quarter. The federal deficit reached record highs through all of 1975 and 1976, and when the last bull market topped out in January 1977, the deficit contracted sharply in the first quarter of the same year.

From the evidence in Figure 13, it looks as if the quarterly federal deficit could be a useful stock market forecaster. Our next job is to develop specific trading rules for playing the market averages with changes in the federal deficit. Here are two trading rules that have worked profitably on the 1965–1977 market averages:

> BUY *when the quarterly federal accounts change from a surplus to a deficit OR when any quarterly deficit increases by at least 30 percent over the average of the two most recent deficits.*

> SELL *(or sell short) when the quarterly federal accounts change from a deficit to a surplus OR when any quarterly deficit contracts by at least 30 percent from the average of the two most recent deficits.*

Table 23 shows the profits that would have been earned by the player who traded the 1965–1977 market averages with these two rules. Returns would have averaged 11.5 percent per year for the player who traded both sides of the

TABLE 23
Purchases and sales with Predictor 11
(1965–1977).

Purchases	Sales
91.39 (October 1965)	93.32 (January 1966)
77.13 (October 1966)	103.76 (October 1968)
85.95 (April 1970)	108.81 (April 1972)
118.42 (January 1973)	110.27 (April 1973)
72.56 (January 1975)	99.05 (April 1977)
93.74 (October 1977)	91.00 (December 1977)

Long positions: 84 months   Total return: 89.95%
Short positions: 72 months   Total return: 59.12%

Annual return: 11.5% per year
12.9% per year—long side only

market, and annual returns would have averaged 12.9 percent for players who traded the long side of the market only. Both returns are superior rates of profit on capital investment. One final point. By our trading rules the player would have been short of the market from January to October 1965, and he would have lost about five points on the transaction. This transaction is not shown in Table 23 because it's awkward to begin a table with a short sale, but the loss from January to October 1965 has been averaged into the rates of return.

Table 24 presents a brief demonstration of our trading rules with real data for stock prices and quarterly federal deficits. We start in 1968, with stock prices at 95.04 and a buy signal in force from the last quarter of 1967. The federal accounts for the first quarter of 1968 showed a deficit of $9.7 billion. Since this is not 30 percent less than the average deficit for the last two quarters of 1967, the buy signal remained in force. The deficit for the second quarter of 1968 was $12 billion dollars—not a significant change—and we held our long positions. However, the third-quarter accounts for 1968 showed a deficit of only $2.3 billion. This was a 79 percent contraction from the average $10.85 billion deficit

TABLE 24

Demonstration of buy and sell signals
with Predictor 11 (36 months).

Month	Stock Prices	Federal Deficits (in billions)
Jan. (1968)	95.04	
Feb.	90.75	
March	89.09 SELL	−$9.7
April	95.67	
May	97.87	
June	100.53 BUY	−12.0
July	100.30	
August	98.11	
Sept.	101.34 SELL	− 2.3
Oct.	103.76	
Nov.	105.40	
Dec.	106.48	+ .7
Jan. (1969)	102.04	
Feb.	101.46	
March	99.30	+11.2
April	101.26	
May	104.62	
June	99.14	+12.0
July	94.71	
August	94.18	
Sept.	94.51	+ 6.7
Oct.	95.52	
Nov.	96.21	
Dec.	91.11	+ 4.2
Jan. (1970)	90.31	
Feb.	87.16	
March	88.65	− 1.1
April	85.95	
May	76.06	
June	75.59 BUY	−12.8
July	75.72	
August	77.92	
Sept.	82.58	−14.6
Oct.	84.37	
Nov.	84.28	
Dec.	90.05	−20.1

of the two previous quarters, and we sold at 103.76 in October 1968, two months before the top of the 1967–1968 bull market.

For the last quarter of 1968 and all four quarters of 1969, the federal accounts reported surpluses. Thus, the sell signal remained in force through each of these five quarters, and we stayed short of the 1969 bear market. At the end of the first quarter of 1970, the federal-accounts indicator was back on the minus side with a small deficit of $1.1 billion. Since a change from surplus to deficit defines a buy signal, we bought into the market in April 1970 with the S&P 500 at 85.95. The bear market had only one more month to fall. This is a good forecasting record for the 1967–1970 market cycle, and Predictor 11 has done almost as well on the other market cycles of the last 13 years.

Future Prospects for Predictor 11

I am more optimistic about the future forecasting power of Predictor 11, along with Predictors 1 and 9, than about any other market indicator. Large federal deficits will probably continue to give greater purchasing power to the individuals and institutions who are most likely to buy stocks, while small deficits will force money away from stocks for the purpose of meeting tax obligations. Since quarterly changes in federal accounts have sometimes approached $35 billion, Predictor 11 deals with large amounts of money, amounts that can really move the market averages around in a two- or three-month period. So while the general relationship between federal accounts and stock prices may be partly correlational, there is probably a strong and direct causal effect of accounts on the market averages.

A second reason for optimism about the continued forecasting power of Predictor 11 follows from the relationship of the federal-accounts indicator to interest rates and inflation. Higher interest rates and higher inflation have accompanied each of the last three bear markets, and both of these conditions tend to encourage lower federal deficits. In the case of credit, for example, the position of the United States government is much like that of any other large institutional borrower. If credit is extremely tight, the treasury will not pay exorbitant interest rates to borrow money that it can otherwise raise through direct taxation. However, borrowing may be more advantageous to the federal government than direct taxation when credit is cheap. Hence, the overall relationship between changing federal accounts and the market averages is probably moderated by what we have already learned about short-term interest rates and stock price changes. Inflation may also be involved in the future forecasting prospects of Predictor 11. For example, the government has several reasons to want to reduce the discretionary income of certain individuals and groups during periods of higher inflation and lower industrial production. Under these circumstances, increasing direct taxation will lower the deficit, reduce the rate of inflation, and draw additional money out of stocks. These are only two of the reasons why I expect Predictor 11 to sustain its forecasting power into the future.

To this point, our analysis has been limited to understanding the relationship between federal accounts and stock prices in terms of taxes, interest rates, and inflation. The other side of the accounts picture, of course, is federal spending. Any effort to relate spending to stock prices is an extremely complicated business, but the really alert market player should consider every circumstance that might distort the forecasting power of his indicators. In the case of federal spending, I suspect that the questions relevant to stock price forecasting have less to do with total amounts of spending than with specific types of spending. For example, does the federal dollar spent on national defense have the same impact on the stock market as the dollar spent on foreign aid? Do expenditures for scientific research affect the market in the same way as federal subsidies to farmers? The answer to both questions is probably no. The market player who is really determined to win his game might want to examine different categories of federal spending as stock price fore-casters. There could very well be additional profits from this type of research effort.

As with every market indicator, the specific trading rules for Predictor 11 are probably less stable than the general relationship between federal accounts and stock prices. There is no guarantee that 30 percent changes in quarterly deficits will always distinguish between future bull and bear market swings, but I would be surprised if the 30 percent standard changes much in the next two or three market cycles. Yet, given the enormous size of the federal deficits in 1975 and 1976, the player might do well to adopt trading rules based on quarterly changes of 35 or 40 percent. A second possibility would be to define trading rules for Predictor 11 in terms of moving averages in federal accounts rather than percentage changes. For the player who wants to develop his own trading rules for Predictor 11, the necessary data for 1965–1977 appear in the Appendix.

Recency and Availability of Data for Predictor 11

Figures for the last quarter's federal accounts are available a week or two after the end of the quarter. Data are published in *Economic Indicators* and the *Survey of Current Business,* monthly publications that are available at most libraries. The earliest figures after the end of the quarter appear first in the daily financial press (for example, *The Wall Street Journal*). There are occasional revisions of the federal accounts series, but the revisions are always minor and can be ignored for stock forecasting purposes.

Federal expenditures are planned and announced well in advance of the fiscal year, and the market player can obtain preliminary estimates of the quarterly deficit several quarters ahead. However, these estimates vary in their reliability, and there is probably no benefit to buying or selling the market before the end of the fiscal quarter in any case. Finally, data on quarterly account deficits and surpluses are also available from the United States Office of the Budget.

2 / Putting It All Together: Comprehensive Market Forecasting

NOW that you have learned to use the 11 predictors of the changing market averages, it is time to demonstrate the forecasting accuracy of all the indicators at the same time. No indicator stands alone, and one, two, or three indicators can often fail together. But the chances of all 11 predictors failing at the same time are exceedingly slim. Table 25, which appears at the end of this chapter, presents a month-by-month forecasting demonstration with all predictors for 156 months. I believe this is one of the longest and most comprehensive records of market forecasting to be published anywhere.

Once you have looked at Table 25, it should be clear that changes in the market averages are closely related to the number of predictors signaling each type of forecast. The market averages usually advance when a majority of the indicators give buy signals, and they usually decline when the majority of indicators give sell signals.

A method of market trading that uses all of the predictors might be almost as profitable as trading with the one or two most profitable predictors. In addition, the risk in using all 11 indicators would also be considerably less than the risk of using only one or two indicators, because 11 predictors are not likely to fail at the same time. Accordingly, a method of comprehensive market forecasting with all 11 predictors could offer the most profitable strategy for the market player who is concerned about losses when his two or three "pet" indicators fail at the same time. Here are the two trading rules for comprehensive market forecasting:

> BUY *when the majority of the predictors forecast a market advance.*
>
> SELL *(or sell short) when the majority of the predictors forecast a market decline.*

Since gold did not trade freely until the middle of 1972, there are only ten predictors from 1965 to 1972. So we also need a rule for months when the predictors split evenly between bull market and bear market forecasts. In the case of ties, it is best to consider the new signal to be the opposite of the signal for the previous month. In other words, if the previous month's forecast was bullish, then this month's tie is a sell signal. But if last month's forecast was bearish, then this month's tie defines a buy signal.

Table 26 shows the profits that would have been made by the player who followed the trading rules of comprehensive market forecasting from 1965 through 1977. Annual profits would have been 12.4 percent for trading both sides of the market and 12.1 percent for trading the long side of the market only. These rates of profit compare favorably with the profits of using only the one or two best predictors, and

TABLE 26
Purchases and sales with comprehensive market forecasting (1965–1977).

Purchases	Sales
86.12 (January 1965)	92.69 (February 1966)
87.36 (February 1967)	95.67 (April 1968)
100.53 (June 1968)	102.04 (January 1969)
75.72 (July 1970)	112.42 (March 1973)
80.10 (February 1975)	99.05 (April 1977)
99.23 (June 1977)	96.23 (September 1977)

Long positions: 97 months	Total return: 97.9%
Short positions: 59 months	Total return: 63.4%

Annual return: 12.4% per year
12.1% per year—long side only

the risks are greatly reduced. Note, for example, that a profit was made on all but one of the six purchases shown in Table 26. Profits were also realized from five of the six short sales. The only loss in the entire 13-year period was less than five points on the two-month short sale between April and June 1968.

Now let's check the timing of comprehensive market forecasting for each major market cycle since 1965. The purchase in January 1965 bought us into the last year of a great bull market which started two years earlier. The sale in February 1966 occurred one month after the January 1966 market top. The purchase in February 1967 was four months after the October bottom of the 1966 market break. In April 1968 there was a false sell signal for the 1967–1968 bull market, but it corrected itself in June 1968, only two months later. The sale in January 1969 was one month after the market top of December 1968, and the purchase in July 1970 coincided exactly with the bottom of the 1969–1970 bear market. The sale in March 1973 was transacted only two months after January 1973, the top of the greatest bull market in history. Finally, our last purchase, in February 1975, occurred two months after the market bottom of December 1974. And we sold out three months after the January 1977 market top.

In summary, this method of comprehensive forecasting consistently sold us out a month or two after four major bull market tops. The same method then bought us into the market within two to four months of three major bear market bottoms. This is probably as close to ideal market forecasting as we are ever likely to come.

FUTURE PROSPECTS FOR COMPREHENSIVE MARKET FORECASTING

This system of market forecasting will continue its accuracy into future market cycles. It may not catch the tops and bottoms of future market cycles quite as closely as it has in the past, but it will certainly continue to bring superior profits to players who follow the trading rules for buying and selling.

The professional market player will do even better if he begins his own research on these predictors in future market cycles. It would be astonishing if all 11 of our predictors failed at the same time, but it would also be surprising if each of the 11 indicators predicted the future as well as it has predicted the past. Ten, twenty, perhaps thirty years from now at least two or three of these predictors will have completely lost their forecasting power, and the most profitable trading rules will certainly have changed for the predictors that still survive. This uncertainty about future market cycles is itself an important certainty. No two markets are exactly alike. The purpose of this book has been to describe several predictors which have consistently and accurately forecast the market averages through three complete market cycles in the last 13 years, but this does not provide any guarantee in itself that each of the 11 predictors will accurately forecast future market cycles. Comprehsnsive market forecasting does *not* assume that future market cycles will mirror previous market cycles in every detail. What it does assume is that the predictors of previous market cycles will forecast future cycles more accurately than any other method of prediction. I presently estimate this accuracy at 80 percent or 85 percent, and the professional market player can take many steps to ensure this level of accuracy in the years ahead.

First, the committed player should follow each predictor through future market cycles. When the forecasting power of any predictor becomes distorted, he should not hesitate to drop that predictor from his forecasting equations.

Second, the winning player will always be looking for new trading rules which can improve the profitability of each predictor's market forecasting. The general relationship between any specific predictors and the market average may continue through many complete market cycles, but the best trading rules for the same predictor could change every two or three cycles. The professional trader will recognize this possibility and revise his trading rules to accord with the specific relationship between each predictor and changing stock prices during the last two or three market cycles.

Finally, the professional will continuously be on the lookout for new predictors. At any time, an economic series believed to have little or no forecasting value may have accurately predicted stock prices in the last two or three market cycles. If the indicator can be tied to stock prices on the basis of sound reasoning and a profitable forecasting record for the last ten years or so, the player will have developed a new predictor.

TABLE 25
Market changes for the S&P 500.

Month	Three Months Later	Six Months Later	Nine Months Later
January 1965 (86.12) Bull Market Predictors: 1, 2, 3, 4, 5, 6, 7, 8, 10 Bear Market Predictors: 11	+1.85	−1.21	+5.27
February 1965 (86.75) Bull Market Predictors: 1, 2, 3, 4, 5, 6, 7, 8, 10 Bear Market Predictors: 11	+3.16	−.26	+5.14
March 1965 (86.83) Bull Market Predictors: 1, 2, 3, 4, 5, 6, 7, 8, 10 Bear Market Predictors: 11	−1.79	+1.41	+4.90
April 1965 (87.97) Bull Market Predictors: 1, 2, 3, 4, 5, 6, 7, 8, 10 Bear Market Predictors: 11	−3.06	+3.42	+4.90
May 1965 (87.28) Bull Market Predictors: 1, 2, 3, 5, 6, 7, 8, 10 Bear Market Predictors: 4, 11	−2.79	+2.87	+3.41
June 1965 (85.04) Bull Market Predictors: 1, 2, 4, 5, 6, 7, 8, 10 Bear Market Predictors: 3, 11	+4.34	+6.69	+3.84
July 1965 (84.91) Bull Market Predictors: 1, 2, 4, 5, 6, 7, 8, 10 Bear Market Predictors: 3, 11	+6.48	+8.41	+6.69
August 1965 (86.49) Bull Market Predictors: 1, 2, 5, 6, 7, 10 Bear Market Predictors: 3, 4, 8, 11	+5.66	+6.20	+.39
September 1965 (89.38) Bull Market Predictors: 1, 2, 4, 5, 6, 10 Bear Market Predictors: 3, 7, 8, 11	+2.35	−.50	−3.32
October 1965 (91.39) Bull Market Predictors: 1, 2, 4, 5, 6, 10 Bear Market Predictors: 3, 7, 8, 11	+1.93	+.21	−5.55

Month	Three Months Later	Six Months Later	Nine Months Later
November 1965 (92.39) Bull Market Predictors: 1, 2, 4, 5, 6, 8, 10 Bear Market Predictors: 3, 7, 11	+.54	−5.37	−11.50
December 1965 (91.73) Bull Market Predictors: 1, 2, 4, 6, 8, 10 Bear Market Predictors: 3, 5, 7, 11	−2.85	−5.67	−13.92
January 1966 (93.32) Bull Market Predictors: 1, 2, 4, 6, 7, 8 Bear Market Predictors: 3, 5, 10, 11	−1.72	−7.48	−16.12
February 1966 (92.69) Bull Market Predictors: 1, 2, 4, 7, 8 Bear Market Predictors: 3, 5, 6, 10, 11	−5.91	−12.04	−11.70
March 1966 (88.88) Bull Market Predictors: 1, 2, 4, 7, 8 Bear Market Predictors: 3, 5, 6, 10, 11	−2.82	−11.07	−7.35
April 1966 (91.60) Bull Market Predictors: 1, 8 Bear Market Predictors: 2, 3, 4, 5, 6, 7, 10, 11	−5.76	−14.47	−7.15
May 1966 (86.78) Bull Market Predictors: 1, 8 Bear Market Predictors: 2, 3, 4, 5, 6, 7, 10, 11	−6.13	−5.79	+.58
June 1966 (86.06) Bull Market Predictors: 1, 4, 7, 8 Bear Market Predictors: 2, 3, 5, 6, 10, 11	−8.25	−4.73	+3.36
July 1966 (85.84) Bull Market Predictors: 1, 7 Bear Market Predictors: 2, 3, 4, 5, 6, 8, 10, 11	−8.71	−1.37	+5.12
August 1966 (80.65) Bull Market Predictors: 1, 7 Bear Market Predictors: 2, 3, 4, 5, 6, 8, 10, 11	+.34	+6.71	+11.94
September 1966 (77.81) Bull Market Predictors: 1 Bear Market Predictors: 2, 3, 4, 5, 6, 7, 8, 10, 11	+3.52	+11.61	+13.62
October 1966 (77.13) Bull Market Predictors: 1 Bear Market Predictors: 2, 3, 4, 5, 6, 7, 8, 10, 11	+7.32	+13.83	+15.88
November 1966 (80.99) Bull Market Predictors: 1, 6 Bear Market Predictors: 2, 3, 4, 5, 7, 8, 10, 11	+6.37	+11.60	+13.50
December 1966 (81.33) Bull Market Predictors: 1, 4, 6 Bear Market Predictors: 2, 3, 5, 7, 8, 10, 11	+8.09	+10.10	+14.48
January 1967 (84.45) Bull Market Predictors: 1, 4, 6, 8 Bear Market Predictors: 2, 3, 5, 7, 10, 11	+6.21	+8.56	+11.21
February 1967 (87.36) Bull Market Predictors: 1, 4, 5, 6, 7, 8 Bear Market Predictors: 2, 3, 10, 11	+5.23	+7.13	+5.30
March 1967 (89.42) Bull Market Predictors: 1, 3, 4, 5, 6, 7, 8, 10 Bear Market Predictors: 2, 11	+2.01	+6.39	+5.88
April 1967 (90.96) Bull Market Predictors: 1, 3, 4, 5, 6, 7, 8, 10, 11 Bear Market Predictors: 2	+2.05	+4.70	+4.08

TABLE 25 (*Continued*)

Month	Three Months Later	Six Months Later	Nine Months Later
May 1967 (92.59) Bull Market Predictors: 1, 3, 4, 5, 6, 8, 10, 11 Bear Market Predictors: 2, 7	+1.90	+2.71	+.07
June 1967 (91.43) Bull Market Predictors: 1, 2, 3, 4, 5, 6, 8, 10, 11 Bear Market Predictors: 7	+4.38	+3.87	−2.34
July 1967 (93.01) Bull Market Predictors: 1, 2, 3, 4, 5, 6, 8, 10, 11 Bear Market Predictors: 7	+2.65	+2.03	+2.66
August 1967 (94.49) Bull Market Predictors: 1, 2, 3, 4, 5, 6, 8, 10, 11 Bear Market Predictors: 7	−1.83	−3.74	+3.38
September 1967 (95.81) Bull Market Predictors: 1, 2, 3, 4, 5, 6, 7, 8, 10, 11 Bear Market Predictors:	−.51	−6.72	+4.72
October 1967 (95.66) Bull Market Predictors: 1, 2, 3, 4, 5, 6, 7, 8, 10, 11 Bear Market Predictors:	−.62	+.01	+4.64
November 1967 (92.66) Bull Market Predictors: 1, 2, 3, 4, 5, 6, 7, 8, 10, 11 Bear Market Predictors:	−1.89	+5.21	+5.45
December 1967 (95.30) Bull Market Predictors: 1, 2, 3, 4, 5, 6, 7, 8, 10, 11 Bear Market Predictors:	−6.21	+5.23	+6.04
January 1968 (95.04) Bull Market Predictors: 1, 2, 3, 4, 5, 6, 7, 8, 10, 11 Bear Market Predictors:	+.63	+5.26	+8.72
February 1968 (90.75) Bull Market Predictors: 1, 2, 3, 4, 5, 6, 7, 8, 10, 11 Bear Market Predictors:	+7.12	+7.36	+14.65
March 1968 (89.09) Bull Market Predictors: 1, 2, 3, 5, 6, 7, 8, 10, 11 Bear Market Predictors: 4	+11.44	+12.25	+17.39
April 1968 (95.67) Bull Market Predictors: 1, 3, 6, 7, 10 Bear Market Predictors: 2, 4, 5, 8, 11	+4.63	+8.09	+6.37
May 1968 (97.87) Bull Market Predictors: 1, 3, 4, 6, 10 Bear Market Predictors: 2, 5, 7, 8, 11	+.24	+7.53	+3.59
June 1968 (100.53) Bull Market Predictors: 1, 2, 3, 4, 6, 8, 10 Bear Market Predictors: 5, 7, 11	+.81	+5.95	−1.23
July 1968 (100.30) Bull Market Predictors: 1, 4, 6, 8, 10, 11 Bear Market Predictors: 2, 3, 5, 7	+3.46	+1.74	+.96
August 1968 (98.11) Bull Market Predictors: 1, 6, 7, 8, 10, 11 Bear Market Predictors: 2, 3, 4, 5	+7.29	+2.35	+6.51
September 1968 (101.34) Bull Market Predictors: 1, 6, 7, 8, 10, 11 Bear Market Predictors: 2, 3, 4, 5	+5.14	−2.04	−2.20
October 1968 (103.76) Bull Market Predictors: 1, 2, 4, 6, 7, 10 Bear Market Predictors: 3, 5, 8, 11	−1.72	−2.50	−9.05

Month	Three Months Later	Six Months Later	Nine Months Later
November 1968 (105.40) Bull Market Predictors: 1, 2, 3, 4, 6, 7, 8, 10 Bear Market Predictors: 5, 11	−3.96	−.78	−11.22
December 1968 (106.48) Bull Market Predictors: 1, 2, 3, 4, 6, 7, 8, 10 Bear Market Predictors: 5, 11	−7.12	−7.34	−11.97
January 1969 (102.04) Bull Market Predictors: 2, 3, 4, 8, 10 Bear Market Predictors: 1, 5, 6, 7, 11	−.78	−7.33	−6.48
February 1969 (101.46) Bull Market Predictors: 2, 3, 4, 8, 10 Bear Market Predictors: 1, 5, 6, 7, 11	+3.16	−7.28	−5.25
March 1969 (99.30) Bull Market Predictors: 2, 3, 7, 10 Bear Market Predictors: 1, 4, 5, 6, 8, 11	−.16	−4.69	−8.19
April 1969 (101.26) Bull Market Predictors: Bear Market Predictors: 1, 2, 3, 4, 5, 6, 7, 8, 10, 11	−6.55	−5.74	−10.95
May 1969 (104.62) Bull Market Predictors: Bear Market Predictors: 1, 2, 3, 4, 5, 6, 7, 8, 10, 11	−6.44	−8.41	−17.46
June 1969 (99.14) Bull Market Predictors: Bear Market Predictors: 1, 2, 3, 4, 5, 6, 7, 8, 10, 11	−4.63	−8.03	−10.49
July 1969 (94.71) Bull Market Predictors: 8 Bear Market Predictors: 1, 2, 3, 4, 5, 6, 7, 10, 11	+.81	−4.20	−8.76
August 1969 (94.18) Bull Market Predictors: 7 Bear Market Predictors: 1, 2, 3, 4, 5, 6, 8, 10, 11	+2.03	−7.02	−18.12
September 1969 (94.51) Bull Market Predictors: 7 Bear Market Predictors: 1, 2, 3, 4, 5, 6, 8, 10, 11	−3.40	−5.86	−18.92
October 1969 (95.56) Bull Market Predictors: 7 Bear Market Predictors: 1, 2, 3, 4, 5, 6, 8, 10, 11	−5.21	−9.57	−19.80
November 1969 (96.21) Bull Market Predictors: 4 Bear Market Predictors: 1, 2, 3, 5, 6, 7, 8, 10, 11	−9.04	−20.15	−18.28
December 1969 (91.11) Bull Market Predictors: 4 Bear Market Predictors: 1, 2, 3, 5, 6, 7, 8, 10, 11	−2.46	−15.52	−8.53
January 1970 (90.31) Bull Market Predictors: 4, 8 Bear Market Predictors: 1, 2, 3, 5, 6, 7, 10, 11	−4.36	−14.59	−5.94
February 1970 (87.16) Bull Market Predictors: 7 Bear Market Predictors: 1, 2, 3, 4, 5, 6, 8, 10, 11	−10.10	−9.24	−2.88
March 1970 (88.65) Bull Market Predictors: 7 Bear Market Predictors: 1, 2, 3, 4, 5, 6, 8, 10, 11	−13.06	−6.07	+1.40
April 1970 (85.95) Bull Market Predictors: 5 Bear Market Predictors: 1, 2, 3, 4, 6, 7, 8, 10, 11	−10.23	−1.58	+7.54
May 1970 (76.06) Bull Market Predictors: 5 Bear Market Predictors: 1, 2, 3, 4, 6, 7, 8, 10, 11	+1.86	+8.22	+21.05

TABLE 25 (*Continued*)

Month	Three Months Later	Six Months Later	Nine Months Later
June 1970 (75.59) Bull Market Predictors: 2, 5, 7, 10 Bear Market Predictors: 1, 3, 4, 6, 8, 11	+6.99	+14.46	+24.01
July 1970 (75.72) Bull Market Predictors: 2, 5, 8, 10, 11 Bear Market Predictors: 1, 3, 4, 6, 7	+8.65	+17.77	+30.32
August 1970 (77.92) Bull Market Predictors: 2, 3, 4, 5, 8, 10, 11 Bear Market Predictors: 1, 6, 7	+6.36	+19.19	+23.72
September 1970 (82.58) Bull Market Predictors: 2, 3, 4, 5, 6, 8, 10, 11 Bear Market Predictors: 1, 7	+7.49	+17.02	+17.14
October 1970 (84.37) Bull Market Predictors: 1, 3, 4, 5, 6, 7, 8, 10, 11 Bear Market Predictors: 2	+9.12	+18.67	+14.63
November 1970 (84.28) Bull Market Predictors: 1, 3, 4, 5, 6, 7, 8, 10, 11 Bear Market Predictors: 2	+12.83	+17.36	+12.96
December 1970 (90.05) Bull Market Predictors: 1, 2, 3, 4, 5, 7, 8, 10, 11 Bear Market Predictors: 6	+9.55	+9.67	+9.35
January 1971 (93.49) Bull Market Predictors: 1, 2, 3, 4, 5, 7, 8, 10, 11 Bear Market Predictors: 6	+9.55	+5.51	+3.80
February 1971 (97.11) Bull Market Predictors: 1, 2, 3, 5, 6, 7, 8, 10, 11 Bear Market Predictors: 4	+4.53	+.13	−4.33
March 1971 (99.60) Bull Market Predictors: 1, 2, 3, 4, 5, 6, 7, 8, 10, 11 Bear Market Predictors:	+.12	−.20	−.43
April 1971 (103.04) Bull Market Predictors: 1, 2, 3, 4, 5, 6, 8, 10, 11 Bear Market Predictors: 7	−4.04	−5.75	+.26
May 1971 (101.64) Bull Market Predictors: 1, 2, 3, 5, 6, 8, 10, 11 Bear Market Predictors: 4, 7	−4.40	−8.86	+3.60
June 1971 (99.72) Bull Market Predictors: 1, 2, 3, 5, 6, 8, 10, 11 Bear Market Predictors: 4, 7	−.32	−.55	+7.97
July 1971 (99.00) Bull Market Predictors: 1, 2, 3, 5, 6, 8, 10, 11 Bear Market Predictors: 4, 7	−1.71	+4.30	+9.81
August 1971 (97.24) Bull Market Predictors: 1, 2, 3, 5, 6, 7, 8, 10, 11 Bear Market Predictors: 4	−4.46	+8.00	+10.41
September 1971 (99.40) Bull Market Predictors: 1, 2, 3, 5, 6, 7, 8, 10, 11 Bear Market Predictors: 4	−.23	+8.29	+8.61
October 1971 (97.29) Bull Market Predictors: 1, 3, 5, 6, 7, 8, 10, 11 Bear Market Predictors: 2, 4	+6.01	+11.52	+9.29
November 1971 (92.78) Bull Market Predictors: 1, 3, 5, 6, 7, 8, 10, 11 Bear Market Predictors: 2, 4	+12.46	+14.87	+18.23

Month	Three Months Later	Six Months Later	Nine Months Later
December 1971 (99.17) Bull Market Predictors: 1, 2, 3, 4, 5, 6, 7, 8, 10, 11 Bear Market Predictors:	+8.52	+8.84	+10.22
January 1972 (103.30) Bull Market Predictors: 1, 2, 3, 4, 5, 6, 7, 8, 10, 11 Bear Market Predictors:	+5.51	+3.91	+6.26
February 1972 (105.24) Bull Market Predictors: 1, 2, 3, 4, 5, 6, 7, 8, 10, 11 Bear Market Predictors:	+2.41	+5.77	+9.81
March 1972 (107.67) Bull Market Predictors: 1, 2, 3, 4, 5, 6, 7, 8, 10, 11 Bear Market Predictors:	+.32	+1.70	+9.81
April 1972 (108.81) Bull Market Predictors: 1, 2, 3, 5, 6, 7, 8, 10, 11 Bear Market Predictors: 4	−1.60	+.75	+0.61
May 1972 (107.65) Bull Market Predictors: 1, 2, 3, 5, 6, 7, 8, 10, 11 Bear Market Predictors: 4	+3.36	+7.40	+6.97
June 1972 (108.01) Bull Market Predictors: 1, 2, 3, 5, 6, 7, 8, 9, 10, 11 Bear Market Predictors: 4	+1.36	+9.49	+4.41
July 1972 (107.21) Bull Market Predictors: 1, 2, 3, 6, 7, 8, 9, 10, 11 Bear Market Predictors: 4, 5	+2.35	+11.21	+3.06
August 1972 (111.01) Bull Market Predictors: 1, 2, ɔ, 6, 7, 8, 10, 11 Bear Market Predictors: 4, 5, 9	+4.04	+3.61	−3.79
September 1972 (109.37) Bull Market Predictors: 1, 2, 3, 6, 7, 8, 10, 11 Bear Market Predictors: 4, 5, 9	+8.11	+3.03	−4.64
October 1972 (109.56) Bull Market Predictors: 1, 2, 3, 4, 6, 7, 8, 9, 10, 11 Bear Market Predictors: 5	+8.86	+.71	−3.73
November 1972 (115.05) Bull Market Predictors: 1, 2, 3, 4, 6, 7, 8, 9, 10, 11 Bear Market Predictors: 5	−.37	−7.83	−11.25
December 1972 (117.50) Bull Market Predictors: 1, 3, 4, 6, 7, 8, 9, 10, 11 Bear Market Predictors: 2, 5	−5.08	−12.75	−11.89
January 1973 (118.42) Bull Market Predictors: 1, 3, 4, 6, 7, 8, 9, 10, 11 Bear Market Predictors: 2, 5	−8.15	−12.59	−8.58
February 1973 (114.62) Bull Market Preuictors: 1, 2, 3, 7, 10, 11 Bear Market Predictors: 4, 5, 6, 8, 9	−7.40	−10.82	−12.59
March 1973 (112.42) Bull Market Predictors: 2, 3, 7, 10, 11 Bear Market Predictors: 1, 4, 5, 6, 8, 9	−7.67	−6.81	−17.64
April 1973 (110.27) Bull Market Predictors: 3, 10 Bear Market Predictors: 1, 2, 4, 5, 6, 7, 8, 9, 11	−4.44	−.43	−14.16
May 1973 (107.22) Bull Market Predictors: 10 Bear Market Predictors: 1, 2, 3, 4, 5, 6, 7, 8, 9, 11	−3.42	−5.19	−13.77
June 1973 (104.75) Bull Market Predictors: 2 Bear Market Predictors: 1, 3, 4, 5, 6, 7, 8, 9, 10, 11	+.86	−9.97	−7.31

TABLE 25 (*Continued*)

Month	Three Months Later	Six Months Later	Nine Months Later
July 1973 (105.83) Bull Market Predictors: 2 Bear Market Predictors: 1, 3, 4, 5, 6, 7, 8, 9, 10, 11	+4.01	−9.72	−13.37
August 1973 (103.80) Bull Market Predictors: 2 Bear Market Predictors: 1, 3, 4, 5, 6, 7, 8, 9, 10, 11	−1.77	−10.35	−14.13
September 1973 (105.61) Bull Market Predictors: 2, 4, 7, 9 Bear Market Predictors: 1, 3, 5, 6, 8, 10, 11	−10.83	−8.17	−15.82
October 1973 (109.84) Bull Market Predictors: 4, 7, 9 Bear Market Predictors: 1, 2, 3, 5, 6, 8, 10, 11	−13.73	−17.38	−27.02
November 1973 (102.03) Bull Market Predictors: 4 Bear Market Predictors: 1, 2, 3, 5, 6, 7, 8, 9, 10, 11	−8.58	−12.36	−26.00
December 1973 (94.78) Bull Market Predictors: 4 Bear Market Predictors: 1, 2, 3, 5, 6, 7, 8, 9, 10, 11	+2.66	−4.99	−26.67
January 1974 (96.11) Bull Market Predictors: Bear Market Predictors: 1, 2, 3, 4, 5, 6, 7, 8, 9, 10, 11	−3.65	−13.29	−26.67
February 1974 (93.45) Bull Market Predictors: 2, 5, 10 Bear Market Predictors: 1, 3, 4, 6, 7, 8, 9, 11	−3.78	−17.42	−21.71
March 1974 (97.44) Bull Market Predictors: 2, 5 Bear Market Predictors: 1, 3, 4, 6, 7, 8, 9, 10, 11	−7.65	−29.32	−30.37
April 1974 (92.46) Bull Market Predictors: 2. 5. 8 Bear Market Predictors: 1, 3, 4, 6, 7, 9, 10, 11	−9.64	−23.20	−19.90
May 1974 (89.67) Bull Market Predictors: 2, 5, 8 Bear Market Predictors: 1, 3, 4, 6, 7, 9, 10, 11	−13.64	−17.93	−9.57
June 1974 (89.79) Bull Market Predictors: 2 Bear Market Predictors: 1, 3, 4, 5, 6, 7, 8, 9, 10, 11	−21.67	−22.72	−6.01
July 1974 (82.82) Bull Market Predictors: Bear Market Predictors: 1, 2, 3, 4, 5, 6, 7, 8, 9, 10, 11	−13.38	−10.26	+1.90
August 1974 (76.03) Bull Market Predictors: Bear Market Predictors: 1, 2, 3, 4, 5, 6, 7, 8, 9, 10, 11	−4.29	+4.07	+14.07
September 1974 (68.12) Bull Market Predictors: 9 Bear Market Predictors: 1, 2, 3, 4, 5, 6, 7, 8, 10, 11	−1.05	+15.66	+24.28
October 1974 (69.44) Bull Market Predictors: 4, 5, 7, 9 Bear Market Predictors: 1, 2, 3, 6, 8, 10, 11	+3.12	+15.28	+23.05
November 1974 (71.74) Bull Market Predictors: 4, 5, 7, 10 Bear Market Predictors: 1, 2, 3, 6, 8, 9, 11	+8.36	+18.36	+13.97
December 1974 (67.07) Bull Market Predictors: 2, 4, 5 Bear Market Predictors: 1, 3, 6, 7, 8, 9, 10, 11	+16.71	+25.33	+17.60

Month	Three Months Later	Six Months Later	Nine Months Later
January 1975 (72.56) Bull Market Predictors: 2, 4, 5, 10, 11 Bear Market Predictors: 1, 3, 6, 7, 8, 9	+12.16	+19.93	+16.01
February 1975 (80.10) Bull Market Predictors: 1, 2, 4, 5, 7, 9, 10, 11 Bear Market Predictors: 3, 6	+10.00	+5.61	+9.97
March 1975 (83.78) Bull Market Predictors: 1, 2, 4, 5, 7, 8, 9, 10, 11 Bear Market Predictors: 3, 6	+8.62	+.89	+4.92
April 1975 (84.72) Bull Market Predictors: 1, 2, 4, 5, 7, 8, 9, 10, 11 Bear Market Predictors: 3, 6	+7.77	+3.85	+12.14
May 1975 (90.10) Bull Market Predictors: 1, 2, 4, 5, 7, 8, 9, 10, 11 Bear Market Predictors: 3, 6	−4.39	−.03	+10.54
June 1975 (92.49) Bull Market Predictors: 1, 2, 4, 5, 7, 8, 9, 10, 11 Bear Market Predictors: 3, 6	+7.73	+3.70	+8.68
July 1975 (92.49) Bull Market Predictors: 2, 5, 6, 7, 8, 9, 10, 11 Bear Market Predictors: 1, 3, 4	+3.92	+4.37	+9.44
August 1975 (85.71) Bull Market Predictors: 2, 3, 5, 6, 7, 8, 9, 10, 11 Bear Market Predictors: 1, 4	+4.36	+14.93	+15.45
September 1975 (84.67) Bull Market Predictors: 2, 3, 6, 7, 8, 9, 10, 11 Bear Market Predictors: 1, 4, 5	+4.03	+16.41	+17.10
October 1975 (88.57) Bull Market Predictors: 3, 6, 7, 8, 9, 10, 11 Bear Market Predictors: 1, 2, 4, 5	+8.29	+13.36	+15.36
November 1975 (90.07) Bull Market Predictors: 1, 3, 4, 5, 6, 7, 8, 9, 10, 11 Bear Market Predictors: 2	+10.57	+11.09	+13.22
December 1975 (88.70) Bull Market Predictors: 1, 2, 3, 4, 5, 6, 7, 8, 9, 10, 11 Bear Market Predictors:	+12.38	+13.07	+16.75
January 1976 (96.86) Bull Market Predictors: 1, 2, 3, 4, 5, 6, 7, 8, 9, 10, 11 Bear Market Predictors:	+15.07	+7.34	+5.03
February 1976 (100.64) Bull Market Predictors: 1, 2, 3, 4, 5, 6, 7, 8, 9, 10, 11 Bear Market Predictors:	+.52	+2.65	+.54
March 1976 (101.08) Bull Market Predictors: 1, 2, 3, 4, 5, 6, 7, 8, 9, 10, 11 Bear Market Predictors:	+.69	+4.37	+5.42
April 1976 (101.93) Bull Market Predictors: 1, 2, 3, 5, 6, 7, 8, 9, 10, 11 Bear Market Predictors: 4	+2.27	−.04	+.88
May 1976 (101.16) Bull Market Predictors: 1, 2, 3, 5, 6, 7, 8, 9, 10, 11 Bear Market Predictors: 4	+2.13	+.03	−.20
June 1976 (101.77) Bull Market Predictors: 1, 2, 3, 4, 5, 6, 7, 8, 9, 10, 11 Bear Market Predictors:	+3.68	+4.73	−1.20
July 1976 (104.20) Bull Market Predictors: 1, 2, 3, 4, 5, 6, 7, 8, 9, 10, 11 Bear Market Predictors:	−2.31	−1.39	−3.63

TABLE 25 (*Continued*)

Month	Three Months Later	Six Months Later	Nine Months Later
August 1976 (103.29) Bull Market Predictors: 1, 2, 3, 4, 5, 6, 7, 8, 9, 10, 11 Bear Market Predictors:	−2.10	−2.31	−4.53
September 1976 (105.45) Bull Market Predictors: 1, 2, 3, 4, 5, 6, 7, 8, 9, 10, 11 Bear Market Predictors:	+1.05	−4.88	−5.22
October 1976 (101.89) Bull Market Predictors: 1, 2, 3, 4, 5, 6, 7, 8, 9, 10, 11 Bear Market Predictors:	+.92	−2.84	−1.71
November 1976 (101.19) Bull Market Predictors: 1, 2, 3, 4, 5, 6, 7, 8, 9, 10, 11 Bear Market Predictors:	−.23	−2.43	−3.44
December 1976 (106.50) Bull Market Predictors: 1, 2, 3, 4, 5, 6, 7, 8, 9, 10, 11 Bear Market Predictors:	−5.93	−7.27	−10.27
January 1977 (102.81) Bull Market Predictors: 1, 2, 3, 4, 5, 6, 7, 8, 9, 10, 11 Bear Market Predictors:	−3.76	−2.63	−9.07
February 1977 (100.96) Bull Market Predictors: 1, 2, 3, 4, 5, 6, 7, 8, 10, 11 Bear Market Predictors: 9	−2.20	−3.21	−6.68
March 1977 (100.57) Bull Market Predictors: 1, 2, 3, 4, 5, 7, 8, 10, 11 Bear Market Predictors: 6, 9	−1.34	−5.34	−9.57
April 1977 (99.05) Bull Market Predictors: 1, 2, 5, 8, 10 Bear Market Predictors: 3, 4, 6, 7, 9, 11	+1.13	−5.31	−8.80
May 1977 (98.76) Bull Market Predictors: 1, 2, 5, 8, 10 Bear Market Predictors: 3, 4, 6, 7, 9, 11	−1.01	−4.48	−9.78
June 1977 (99.23) Bull Market Predictors: 1, 2, 5, 8, 9, 10 Bear Market Predictors: 3, 4, 6, 7, 11	−3.00	−8.23	−10.41
July 1977 (100.18) Bull Market Predictors: 1, 4, 5, 7, 8, 9, 10 Bear Market Predictors: 2, 3, 6, 11	−6.42	−9.73	−7.47
August 1977 (97.75) Bull Market Predictors: 4, 6, 7, 8, 9, 10 Bear Market Predictors: 1, 2, 3, 5, 11	−3.47	−8.77	−0.34
September 1977 (96.23) Bull Market Predictors: 4, 6, 7, 8, 10 Bear Market Predictors: 1, 2, 3, 5, 9, 11	−5.23	−7.41	+1.43
October 1977 (93.74) Bull Market Predictors: 6, 7, 8, 10, 11 Bear Market Predictors: 1, 2, 3, 4, 5, 9	−3.49	−2.03	+3.45
November 1977 (94.28) Bull Market Predictors: 6, 8, 10, 11 Bear Market Predictors: 1, 2, 3, 4, 5, 7, 9	−5.30	+3.13	−9.64
December 1977 (91.00) Bull Market Predictors: 6, 8, 10, 11 Bear Market Predictors: 1, 2, 3, 4, 5, 7, 9	−2.18	+6.66	+12.86

3 / Selecting Individual Stocks: Six Principles

HAVING learned to use the 11 predictors that forecast the market averages, you must now deal with the problem of selecting individual stocks for purchase and sale. However, there are ways to avoid the problem of individual stock selection. One solution is to buy or sell a portfolio of stocks that corresponds exactly to the Dow-Jones industrial average or the S&P 500. This, of course, is exactly what is already done by the so-called "index" funds, which have recently become quite fashionable on Wall Street.

There is one very important fact you should know before you buy an index fund or design your own portfolio to match any major market index. Years of performance data have proven conclusively that the stock selections of the average manager of mutual funds and trust funds actually perform somewhat worse than the market averages. In other words, if the S&P 500 is down, say, 10 percent for the last six months, the individual stocks purchased by the average Wall Street money manager will be down at least 10 percent, and they will probably be down an average of 12 percent, 13 percent, or 14 percent. And if the market is up 25 percent over a specified time, the average fund manager will be up only 21 percent, 22 percent, or so on his stock purchases for the same time period.

The index fund is simply Wall Street's answer to the problem of worse-than-average investment performance. If the assets of a large mutual fund are invested only in the individual stocks that comprise the Dow-Jones industrial average or the S&P 500, the problem of underperformance is solved. The index fund can neither outperform nor underperform its market average, and since the average money manager can't outperform the market averages in any case, the index fund simply eliminates the risk that he will do worse than the market.

Does an index fund sound like a prescription for mediocrity? Absolutely. But the fact that the Wall Street professionals can't even keep pace with the market averages simply provides one more important reason why you should handle your own investments. When you have finished this chapter, you are going to be able to keep up with the market averages and perhaps do a little better than that.

How important is the selection of individual stocks to winning the stock market game? Before tackling this question, I want you to review Table 1. Remember that 97 of 100 stocks declined in the bear market of 1973–1974, and that 98 of the same 100 stocks advanced in the 1975–1976 bull market. Since virtually all stocks eventually move with the major market swings, there is a second school of thought that avoids the problem of individual stock selection by encouraging the player to randomly buy and sell stocks according to his market forecast. Advocates of random selection argue that since everything goes up in bull markets, the investor will realize a profit on just about any stock he buys. This is true, and it is demonstrated for every bull market when a senator or congressman proves he could have made money by throwing darts at the stock quotations listed in his home town newspaper. Since everything goes down in bear markets, advocates of random selection argue that you can make money by shorting almost any stock.

So why be concerned about the selection of individual stocks if everything eventually moves with the market? There are at least three important reasons. First, no system of forecasting the market averages is perfect. Second, virtually all stocks move with the major swings, but not all stocks will move with intermediate market changes. Third, and most significant, accurate market forecasting and correct stock selection will return much larger profits than market forecasting alone.

How much profit is added by correct stock selection? Let's find out with two hypothetical examples.

First, let us assume that the player starts with $1,000 in January 1973, the peak of the last bull market. Now assume that the player allocates his $1,000 to equal shares of the 100 stocks shown in Table 1 and goes short in January 1973. Twenty-one months later it is October 1974, the 1973–1974 bear market is bottoming out, and the player covers his short sales for a total cost of $470. Ignoring brokers' commissions and dividend payouts on the short sales, the player's profit is $530 ($1,000 − $470 = $530) on the bear market. The player now adds his $530 profit to his original stake of $1,000 and invests his $1,530 in equal shares of 100 stocks shown in Table 1. Two years later, in January 1971, his second investment would have doubled to $3,182, ignoring brokers' commissions and dividends received. In other words, the player would have tripled his original investment in four years with perfect market forecasting and no consideration of individual stock selection.

Now let's see what happens if we add ideal stock selection to perfect market forecasting for the 100 issues in Table 1. Instead of shorting all 100 stocks in January 1973, let's assume the player shorted the ten biggest losers in the 1973–1974 bear market. (These ten stocks were Addressograph-Multigraph, Alberto-Culver, American Air Filter, American Airlines, American Building Maintenance, AMF, Arvin Industries, Avon Products, Bell & Howell, and Berkey Photo.) By October 1974, at the bottom of the bear market, the player could have covered his original $1,000 short sale for $135, for a profit of $865. The player's new stake is now $1,865 ($1,000 + $865), and we will assume the player distributes his entire investment among the ten best-performing stocks from Table 1 during the 1975–1976 bull market. (These stocks were Ambac Industries, American

Bakeries, American Broadcasting, American Standard, Arvin Industries, Avnet, Bache Group, Berkey Photo, Blue Bell, and Boeing.) By January 1977, the player's $1,865 investment in these ten stocks would have sold for $7,671.

Let's compare the two examples. In the first case, perfect market forecasting alone multiplied an original investment of $1,000 to $3,182. In the second case, perfect market forecasting and ideal stock selection increased the same $1,000 investment to $7,671. Ideal stock selection, then, made the difference between a profit of $2,128 or a profit of $6,671 through the same market cycle.

Now let's come back to reality. No more than there is an ideal system of market forecasting will there ever be a perfect system of stock selection. There is no power on earth that would have enabled us to select and sell short the ten issues from the 100 stocks in Table 1 that were heading for the biggest decline in the 1973–1974 bear market. Nor is there any system that would have bought us into the ten largest winners before the start of the 1975–1976 bull market. However, there are principles of stock selection that will help us sell issues that consistently decline farther than the market averages during major bear swings. There are also selection principles for buying issues that consistently outpace the market on bull swings. Just as we can approximate ideal market forecasting with our 11 predictors, we can approximate ideal stock selection with our selection principles for buying and selling. These principles, while far short of perfect, are considerably more profitable than random stock selection or buying an index fund.

PRINCIPLES OF BUYING

Advances of different stocks are more variable in bull markets than the decline of individual stocks in bear markets. No stock can ever lose more than 100 percent of its value in a bear market, but some stocks will double, triple, and quadruple in a bull market while other stocks advance 50 percent or 60 percent and others increase only 10 percent or 20 percent in the same market.

Our task is to develop and apply the selection principles that will enable us to buy stocks that consistently advance farther than the market averages during major bull swings. Of course, there is no principle of stock selection that will enable us to beat the market averages on every single purchase. But if 70 percent or 75 percent of our purchases beat the bull market averages, the profits will still be much greater than the profits from an index fund or from random stock selection. These additional profits are well worth the time and effort required to understand and use each of the three purchasing principles I have developed for bull market forecasts.

Buying Principle 1: Previous Bear Market Decline

Table 1 shows the last bear market low (October 1974) and the most recent bull market high (January 1977) for each of the 100 stocks in our research sample. These 100 stocks advanced an average of 108 percent in the 1975–1976 bull market, and our task is to apply Buying Principle 1 to select a smaller group of stocks which advanced more than 108 percent in the same market.

According to Buying Principle 1, the stocks with the largest declines in the previous bear market offer excellent prospects for the largest advances in the next bull market. There are two reasons for this expectation. First, the biggest losers of the previous bear market are probably more volatile than average. Since volatility works both ways, these stocks are also better-than-average prospects for beating the bull market averages on the upside. Second, bear market pessimism has usually been overdone for many of these stocks. If a stock loses 85 percent, 90 percent, or even 95 percent of its price in a bear market, it could mean that its corporate earnings have fallen, its dividends have been curtailed, that the company's future prospects are nil, and that bankruptcy is just around the corner. A 90 percent or 95 percent decline might indicate serious problems, but it could also simply mean that investors have soured on the stock, although the company's present situation and future prospects aren't really much worse at the end of the bear market than they were at its beginning. If this is the case, many of these big losers of the last bear market are now seriously undervalued, and they will beat the market averages when the next bull market begins.

If Buying Principle 1 is valid, then the stocks which declined most in the last bear market will also advance most sharply in the next bull market. Here's the complete statement of the principle:

> *For bull market forecasts,* BUY *stocks which have declined the most in the previous bear market.*

How well does this principle work in practice? From our research sample of 100 stocks, Table 27 shows the bull market advance for each of the 16 stocks that declined more than 75 percent in the previous bull market. These same 16 stocks enjoyed an average advance of 159 percent in the 1975–1976 bull market, compared to an average advance of 108 percent for all 100 stocks. In other words, these largest losers from the previous bear market advanced almost half again as much as the average stock in the 1975–1976 bull market. Table 27 also shows the percentage advance for each of the 16 stocks, and we can see that 14 stocks did better than the 108 percent average, while two stocks advanced less than the average. Buying Principle 1 was correct in 87 percent of its selections.

If Buying Principle 1 is valid, then reversal of the principle should point out a sample of stocks that consistently advanced less than the 108 percent bull market average. To test this reversal, I took the 14 stocks that declined 30 percent or less in the 1973–1974 bear market. These 14 stocks

TABLE 27
Bull market advances for 16 stocks that declined 75 percent in the previous bear market.

Stock	Bear Market Low October 1974	Bull Market High January 1977	Percent Advance
Addressograph-Multigraph	3	10	233
Alberto-Culver	4	8	100
Alexander's	2	7	250
American Air Filter	5	18	260
American Airlines	4	15	275
American Building Maintenance	4	10	150
American District Telegraph	15	26	73
AMF	9	20	122
Arvin Industries	4	17	325
Associated Dry Goods	13	33	154
Automatic Data Processing	20	58	190
Avon Products	18	38	111
Bache Group	2	8	300
Bell & Howell	8	19	137
Beneficial	11	27	145
Berkey Photo	1	4	300

Average Advance: 159%

advanced an average of only 83 percent in 1975–1976, considerably less than the average advance of 108 percent for all the issues in Table 1.

Future Prospects for Buying Principle 1

Most of the comments I will offer about Selling Principle 3 apply equally to Buying Principle 1. Both principles work because they select individual stocks of higher-than-average volatility, and these are the stocks that consistently rise and fall farther than the market averages. This tendency is reinforced by excessive optimism and speculation in volatile stocks during bull markets and equally excessive pessimism and neglect of the same stocks at the end of major bear markets. I foresee no immediate change in these circumstances, and for this reason I expect Buying Principle 1 to sustain its selection power in future market cycles.

The alert market player should heed warnings against trying to calculate specific indexes of volatility for different stocks. The principle only provides reasonable assurance that the biggest losers of the last bear market will outpace the average stock in the next bull market. The principle does not guarantee that a sample of 50 percent losers from the last bear market will necessarily beat a sample of 40 percent losers in the next bull market. Volatility is only a general concept, and it must be treated as such for purposes of individual stock selection. Specific coefficients of volatility are practically useless for individual price forecasting.

The last question to be considered deals with a problem that affects each of our principles of individual stock selection. The purchasing principles for a bull market forecast are different, of course, from the selling principles for a bear market forecast. Since even the best market forecasting system will occasionally forecast incorrectly, the player will occasionally incur the risk of buying stocks before a market decline and selling before a market advance. The question, then, that must be asked of every selection principle is this: what happens to the player who sells before a market advance or buys before a decline? Does the player simply lose the percentage that the market averages move against him, or does he lose more or less than the averages for having used a particular selection principle? The answer is different for each selection principle; thus each selection principle has a different level of risk for an incorrect market forecast.

The losses that arise from the application of Buying Principle 1 to an incorrect market forecast will be considerable. The player who buys volatile stocks and then finds the market averages declining will certainly incur greater losses than the extent of the market decline. If the bull market forecast is wrong, these stocks will decline farther than average in a general market decline. My best estimate of the additional risk is 25 percent to 30 percent. For example, if the market averages decline 10 percent against the player who has used Buying Principle 1, his individual stock purchases will probably be down an average of 12.5 percent or 13 percent in the same decline. Since the best market forecasting system will be wrong at least 10 percent or 15 percent of the time, the player who uses Buying Principle 1 should be prepared for occasional adversity.

Recency and Availability of Data for Buying Principle 1

Recency presents no problem with this principle. When the market indicators forecast a bull market, the player simply buys a portfolio of the stocks which have declined farthest in the most recent bear market. Since the last bear market may have been in force for several years, the player must obtain the prices for previous bull market tops for each stock in order to calculate the percentage decline in the bear market. This earlier price information is most easily obtained from stock price charts. *Moody's Handbook of Common Stocks,* the *Value Line Investment Survey,* and *Standard & Poor's Stock Guide* are the most accessible sources of charts. Most libraries subscribe to one or more of these publications. Stock splits, stock dividends, and other corporate actions that change stock prices are comparatively rare in bear markets. Therefore, if the player simply obtains a back copy of *The Wall Street Journal* or his local newspaper for the date of the last bull market top, he will find most of the largest bear market losers. I recommend this latter course of action to the player who lacks the time or patience to obtain and read stock price charts.

Buying Principle 2: Small Market Capitalization

The current selling price of a stock represents, for better or worse, the market's present evaluation of the stock's worth. If we take this selling price and multiply it by the total number of shares of the stock, we arrive at the market's total evaluation of the company that issued the stock. Whether the entire corporation is actually worth as much or more (or less) than the market says it's worth is also an important question, but we need not consider it just yet. The important point to remember is that the present selling price of a stock times the total number of shares is the market's current evaluation (or capitalization) of the entire company.

Different companies vary enormously in their market capitalizations. AT&T, for example, is presently capitalized at about $36 billion, and the current capitalization of General Motors is about $19 billion. Most of the nation's larger corporations are capitalized at over $1 billion, but the figure is much lower for many of the smaller companies whose stocks trade on the major exchanges. Buying Principle 2 exploits the consistent relationship between present market capitalization and price action to select stocks that will advance farther than the market averages during major bull markets. This relationship is not complicated: stocks of companies with smaller market capitalizations will advance more than the market averages in bull markets, and stocks of corporations with larger capitalizations will advance less than the market averages in the same bull markets.

Two brief examples may help make this principle easier to understand. First, imagine Company A with one million outstanding shares presently selling for $10 each. The market's present capitalization for Company A is $10 million (one million shares × $10/share). Now if an additional $5 million turns up in the bull market for Company A stock, the capitalization of Company A will increase from $10 million to $15 million. Assuming that no additional stock is issued, the shares of Company A will increase from $10 to $15 apiece, a 50 percent advance. If an additional $10 million turns up in the bull market, the original capitalization of $10 million for Company A will be doubled to $20 million, and each of the one million shares will double from $10 to $20 apiece.

Now let's consider Company B, which has 5 million outstanding shares selling at $10 each. The market presently capitalizes Company B at $50 million (5 million shares ×

$10/share). If an additional $5 million of bull market money turns up for Company B, the capitalization of the company increases from $50 billion to $55 billion. This represents an increase of 15 percent, and each of the 5 million shares will also increase 10 percent, or from $10 to $11 ($55 million + 5 million shares). If an extra $10 million turn up in the bull market, the capitalization of Company B will increase from $50 million to $60 million, and each share will increase from $10 to $12.

To summarize our two examples, $10 million of new money causes the stock of Company A to double, but $10 million causes the stock of Company B to increase only 20 percent. Why? The difference results from the fact that the capitalization of Company B is five times larger than the capitalization of Company A. Therefore it will take five times as much extra money to advance a share of Company B stock to the same amount as a share of Company A stock. Ten million dollars will double the capitalization of Company A, but it would take an extra $50 million to double the capitalization of Company B.

Although this explanation of the principle of capitalization is greatly oversimplified, stocks with smaller capitalizations will advance farthest in bull markets simply because it takes less money to move these stocks. Here's Buying Principle 2:

> *For bull market forecasts,* BUY *stocks with the smallest market capitalization.*

It's time to test the profitability of Buying Principle 2 with real stock price data. The 100 stocks in Table 1 cover the market advance from October 1974 to January 1977, and the average stock in Table 1 advanced 108 percent. To test our purchasing principle, I first calculated the October 1974 market capitalization for each of the 100 stocks on the list. I found that 15 of the 100 corporations were capitalized at $23 million or less in October 1974. Table 28 shows the price advances for these 15 stocks to the January 1977 market top, and the results were excellent. The 15 stocks in Table 28 advanced an average of 175 percent, while the average advance for all 100 stocks was 108 percent in the same bull market. In other words, the stocks of these 15 companies with the smallest capitalizations advanced more than two-thirds again as much as the average advance for all 100 stocks. Notice also that 12 of the 15 stocks beat the average of 108 percent, while three stocks failed to beat the market. Buying Principle 2 did better than average for 80 percent of its selections.

Another way to test the validity of the capitalization principle is to see what happens when the principle is reversed. If stocks with smallest capitalizations advance farthest in a bull market, the stocks with the largest capitalizations should advance least in the same market. To see if this is true, I separated from Table 1 the 19 companies with the largest market

TABLE 28
Bull market advances for 15 stocks with smallest market capitalizations.

Stock	Bear Market Low October 1974	Bull Market High January 1977	Percent Advance
Addressograph-Multigraph	3	10	233
Alberto-Culver	4	8	100
Alexander's	2	7	250
Allied Products	11	15	36
Alpha Portland Industries	6	16	167
Ambac Industries	5	23	360
American Air Filter	5	18	250
American Bakeries	3	12	300
American Building Maintenance	4	10	150
American Hoist & Derrick	7	18	157
Armstrong Rubber	11	24	118
Arvin Industries	4	17	325
Bache Group	2	8	300
Belding Heminway	4	8	100
Berkey Photo	1	4	300

Average Advance: 175%

capitalizations ($500 million or more) in October 1974. At the January 1977 bull market top these 19 stocks had advanced an average of only 61 percent, compared to the average advance of 108 percent for all 100 stocks. Thus, the advance for these 19 stocks was only half the average advance, and it was only about one-third the advance of the 15 stocks with the smallest capitalizations. In addition, all but two (or 17 of 19) of the stocks with the largest capitalizations advanced less than 108 percent in the 1975–1976 bull market, a selection average of 89 percent.

Future Prospects for Buying Principle 2

Stocks with smaller market capitalizations have advanced farther than the averages in every bull market for which we have records, and I have no reason to think that this selection principle will be distorted in future market cycles. The professional market player should validate the purchasing principle for other samples of stocks in other bull markets, but my own evidence indicates that stocks of companies with the smallest capitalizations have consistently advanced about half again as much as the bull market averages. Thinly capitalized stocks advance farther in bull markets simply because it takes less money to move these stocks as far as the stocks of a company that is more generously capitalized. To be sure, the larger company attracts more money than the smaller company in the same bull market, but it does not attract more money in direct proportion to its greater capitalization, and the stocks of the least capitalized companies advance farthest.

In particular, Buying Principle 2 is complicated by several considerations that I have omitted from my analysis. These considerations do not affect the general selection power of the principle, but the professional market player will probably do even better with this principle if his purchases take account of the following considerations. First, different stocks are held by different people and institutions. Some stocks are favorites of speculators, others are favored by mutual

funds, others by trust funds, others are held by small investors who simply buy them and put them away, and still
others are closely held by the families of the original owners.
It follows that the supply of an issue that is available for the
market will always be less than the total number of outstanding shares, and at times this difference will be considerable.
If the player can arrive at reasonably accurate estimates of
the amount of stock that is not presently available for the
market, he can revise his capitalization figures accordingly.
These revised figures would undoubtedly yield more profitable stock selections than the figures for total capitalization.

A second variable that might further improve the profitability of Buying Principle 2 is sales volume of a stock at the
end of the bear market or at the beginning of the bull market. A high ratio of sales to number of outstanding shares indicates that a stock is turning over rapidly. Stocks that com-
bine high turnover with small capitalization will probably
advance farther in bull markets than stocks with small capitalization and lower turnover. Since sales volume for most
issues tends to persist for several months (and sometimes for
years), the player will probably do best to purchase thinly
capitalized stocks with high ratios of sales volume to total
shares at the time of the bull market forecast.

Finally, we must consider the consequences of using Buying Principle 2 for an incorrect market forecast. Unlike volatility, the capitalization principle does not function as a two-
way street. Thinly capitalized stocks don't fall much farther
than the averages in bear markets. The reasons for this lack
of symmetry are too complicated to discuss here, but my
evidence suggests that thinly capitalized stocks will fall only
about 10 percent more than the market averages during
major bear swings. Therefore, the player who buys thinly
capitalized stocks in front of a declining market loss of about
10 percent, for example, will be down about 11 percent on
his individual stock purchases. The risks of using Buying
Principle 2 are much lower than the risks of using the volatility principle. However, neither selection principle can com-

pensate for sloppy market forecasting. The player who uses the 11 indicators of market forecasting will seldom encounter an adverse market move as large as 10 percent.

Recency and Availability of Data for Buying Principle 2

To calculate total market capitalization for a company, the player needs two separate pieces of information: the latest selling price of its stock and the number of outstanding shares. The price information is as recent as today's newspaper or *Wall Street Journal* and just as readily available. The number of shares is affected by stock splits and stock dividends, but these do not change capitalization, because price is adjusted in proportion to the split or dividend. Capitalization is increased only when a company makes a new offering of common stock, and it is decreased only when shares are purchased by the parent company (for retirement) or by a second company (for acquisition). These changes in capitalization are recorded immediately in the subsequent issues of the major stock guides.

Figures for the number of outstanding shares are published in so many sources that I will list only the four publications most easily obtained by the market player: (1) *Moody's Handbook of Common Stocks,* (2) the *Value Line Investment Survey,* (3) *Standard & Poor's Monthly Stock Guide,* and (4) *Standard & Poor's Quarterly Stock Reports.* All but the smallest branch libraries subscribe to at least one of these four publications.

Buying Principle 3:
Selling Price Lower than Quick Assets

The market's present capitalization of any corporation represents a judgment of the value of that company, expressed in dollars. But what is a company really worth? Is it possible to develop a standard of stock valuation that is independent of market valuation? If the answer to this question is yes, then it would also be possible to compare an independent valuation of a company to its present market valuation. The independent valuation of a company might be larger than the market's evaluation of the same company, a case of undervaluation. Or the market's evaluation of a company might be larger than the independent valuation, a case of overvaluation. These two basic ideas, undervaluation and overvaluation, have important consequences for predicting the price advances of individual stocks in bull markets.

Our next problem is to develop a standard or a procedure for calculating an independent appraisal of a company's worth. One traditional accounting procedure is to total all the long-term and short-term assets of a company and to then total the long-term and short-term liabilities of the same company. When total liabilities are subtracted from total assets, the remainder is called net assets. Finally, these net assets are divided by the number of outstanding shares to arrive at a figure that is called the *book value* per share of common stock.

Now it turns out that book value offers very little help in selecting stocks for purchase. In the same bull market, stocks selling for less than their present book values will not necessarily advance farther than stocks selling for more than their book value. The basic problem with the concept of book value is that it is impossible to accurately appraise the value of many long-term corporate assets. A railroad, for example, may carry its diesel engines on the books at $2 million each. But it is nearly impossible to anticipate the selling price of these engines if the company is dissolved and the engines are auctioned off next week. Each engine might fetch half a million dollars, or $1 million, or $3 million; but it is unlikely that the engines will sell for exactly $2 million apiece, the same value that is carried on the books for each engine. The same uncertainty about market worth applies to most long-term corporate assets. The box cars of a railroad, the airplanes of an airline, the patents and laboratories of a drug company, the assembly plants of an auto manufacturer are all cases in point. No one can predict the selling price of these assets with any certainty.

Although book values are practically worthless for selecting stocks, there are two reasons why you should be aware of this concept. First, a couple of highly respected brokerage firms have just "discovered" book value, and they are now busily peddling stocks selling below book value to anyone unwise enough to buy them. Since book value is of little use in selecting stocks, don't be taken in by this latest example of Wall Street huckstering. The second reason you should understand the idea of book value is that a minor adjustment in the calculation of assets and liabilities leads directly to a principle of stock selection which is extraordinarily profitable in bull markets.

The major problem with book value is the problem of appraising long-term corporate assets. So let's forget about long-term assets and recalculate book value as if there were no long-term assets. First, we total the short-term assets, or "quick" assets. From the total quick assets we subtract both the long-term and short-term liabilities. The remainder is called net quick assets. Finally, we divide net quick assets by the number of outstanding shares. In other words, the calculation for net quick assets is the same as the calculation of book value except that long-term assets are ignored.

Now let's get a feel for some general relationships between net quick assets per share and market price per share for the same stock. First, there are certain types of corporations for which net quick assets cannot be calculated. These are primarily banks and insurance companies. Second, there are many corporations for which net quick assets are negative rather than positive. Negative quick assets result when the total of the short-term assets is less than the total of the long-term and short-term liabilities. Just about any type of company can show negative quick assets, but there are certain businesses that invariably have negative quick assets. Utilities, railroads, steel and oil companies, and drug manufacturers are good examples of this type of company. Stocks of companies with no quick assets or negative net quick assets are not eligible for selection with Buying Principle 3, and they are eliminated from further consideration.

These eliminations still leave the great majority of corporations with positive net quick assets, and this brings us to the core of our purchasing principle for bull market forecasts. For most of these companies, the present market price per share will be higher than the net quick assets per share. But there are usually a few companies for which the present market price per share is lower than the net quick assets per share, and it is the stocks of these companies that we should buy when the market indicators forecast a major bull swing.

Why purchase stocks selling for less than their net quick assets? The answer is simple: the market has seriously undervalued these stocks. Short-term assets consist of items like cash on hand, accounts receivable, and immediate inventories, and the values of these short-term assets are just as certain as the values of long-term assets are uncertain. A company with short-term assets large enough to pay off its total liabilities and with enough remaining assets to cover the present market price of its common stock is in excellent financial condition. If the company is dissolved, acquired, or merged, its net quick assets are guaranteed to be worth more than the current selling price of its common stock. Finally, any money that is realized from the sale of the long-term assets is simply another bonus for the shareholders—though we don't have to count on the long-term assets being worth a dime. A stock selling for less than its net quick assets is so undervalued that it is very likely to advance farther in a bull market than the average stock. So here's our third buying principle:

> *For bull market forecasts,* BUY *stocks selling for less than their net quick assets per share.*

Let's check the profitability of our principle among the 100 stocks shown in Table 1 for the 1975–1976 bull market.

First, I calculated the net quick assets per share for each of these stocks. Next, I compared this figure with the market price for each stock at the bear market bottom of October 1974. At that time, 14 of the 100 stocks were selling for less than their net quick assets. Table 29 shows the advances of these 14 stocks in the 1975–1976 bull market. The 14 stocks advanced an average of 211 percent, versus an average advance of 108 percent for all 100 stocks. In other words, these stocks selling below their quick assets advanced almost twice as far as the average stock in the same bull market. Ten of the 14 stocks beat the average of 108 percent, four failed to do so, and the selection average for this sample was 71 percent.

Now let's see what happens if Buying Principle 3 is reversed. First, let's consider stocks with negative net quick assets at the market bottom of October 1974. According to our principle, these stocks should have advanced less than aver-

TABLE 29
Bull market advances for 14 stocks with lowest ratios of price to quick assets.

Stock	Bear Market Low October 1974	Bull Market High January 1977	Percent Advance
Acme-Cleveland	7	13	86
Addressograph-Multigraph	3	10	233
Alberto-Culver	4	8	100
Alco Standard	6	19	216
Ambac Industries	5	23	360
American Building Maintenance	4	10	150
American Sterilizer	11	12	9
Anderson, Clayton	31	101	226
Avnet	4	17	325
Belding Heminway	4	8	100
Bell & Howell	8	19	137
Berkey Photo	1	4	300
Blue Bell	12	59	392
Boeing	11	43	291
Average Advance: 211%			

age in the 1975–1976 bull market. There were 33 (of the 100) companies with negative net quick assets in October 1974. The stocks of these companies gained an average of 102 percent in the bull market, compared to the average of 108 percent for all 100 stocks. This is only a minor difference, but 23 of these 33 stocks advanced less than the 108 percent, while 10 stocks did better than 108 percent. The reversal was successful in about 70 percent of its selections.

A second way of reversing Buying Principle 3 would be to consider companies that have positive net quick assets but whose stocks are selling for much more than the values of their assets. These stocks with highest ratio of market prices to net quick assets should also advance less than average in bull markets. To check this possibility, I took a sample of 11 stocks from Table 1 that were selling for at least seven times as much as their net quick assets per share in October 1974. These 11 stocks advanced an average of 62 percent in the 1975–1976 bull market, compared to an average advance of 108 percent for all 100 stocks. Moreover, none of these 11 stocks advanced more than the average of 108 percent.

Future Prospects for Buying Principle 3

Stocks selling on the market for prices lower than their net quick assets are excellent bargains at the end of any bear market. This statement even applies to the long bear market of the 1930s; the stock selling farthest below their quick assets in the Great Depression also advanced the farthest when the market finally recovered.

The distinguished security analyst Benjamin Graham maintained careful records for the price advances of stocks selling below quick assets in the bull markets of the 1940s and 1950s. These stocks consistently beat the bull market average, and as an extra bonus, they consistently declined less than the market averages in the bear markets of the same period. The historical record for buying stocks selling below their net quick assets is so persuasive that I am confident of continued profitability in future bull markets.

Although the selection principle is sound, an occasional problem for the contemporary market player is to find enough issues selling below their quick assets. This is not a problem at the end of major bear markets, when as many as 10 percent to 15 percent of all listed stocks are selling below their net quick assets. But if the bull market forecast follows anything other than a major bear market, stocks selling below their quick assets will be scarce. If the bull market still has farther to go and the player can't find stocks selling for less than quick assets, I recommend that he buy stocks selling for less than 1.5 times their net quick assets.

My research also indicates that the player can further increase the profitability of Buying Principle 3 with one additional strategy. Since stocks selling below net quick assets are fairly plentiful at major bear market bottoms, the player who receives a bull market forecast at this time can pick and choose among many undervalued stocks. Instead of simply buying stocks selling for less than their net quick assets, he can restrict his purchases to stocks selling for less than half or less than three-quarters of their net quick assets. A selling price of less than half the net quick assets is extremely low, and only a few stocks will fall this far in the worst bear markets. But the player who finds these few stocks will probably do even better than 211 percent on his purchases before the next bull market tops out.

Finally, Buying Principle 3 is our only principle of stock selection that actually cuts the losses of the player who acts on an incorrect market forecast. Stocks selling for the lowest ratios of price to net quick assets not only advance farthest in bull markets, but they decline least in bear markets. Even at bull market tops, stocks with low ratios of price to quick assets are seriously undervalued relative to other issues. These stocks will decline in a major bear swing, of course, but they will consistently decline less than the bear market averages. How much less? My own research places the figure at 40 percent less. For example, the player who buys these stocks and then finds the market averages declining 10 percent against his position will be down only about 6 percent on his purchases.

I always recommend putting market forecasting ahead of stock selection, but Buying Principle 3 is the exception that proves the rule. I have no doubt that a competent security analyst could use only Buying Principle 3, ignore market forecasting altogether, and still finish well ahead of the game. His losses in bear markets would be comparatively small, and they would be easily offset by his much larger profits in bull markets. Of course, the same player would do even better with reasonably accurate market forecasting, but savings in time, energy, and patience may well be adequate compensation for the extra profits forgone, at least for some players. If you simply must play the market without adequate market forecasting, you can still finish ahead if you follow this purchasing principle.

Recency and Availability of Data for Buying Principle 3

Calculations for this principle require two sets of data: current stock prices and net quick assets per share. The stock prices may be obtained from any recent issue of *The Wall Street Journal* or your local newspaper. Net quick assets per share can be calculated from any stock guide that presents information on each corporation's financial position. The four stock guides most accessible to the market player are *Moody's Handbook of Common Stocks,* the *Value Line Investment Survey, Standard & Poor's Monthly Stock Guide,* and *Standard & Poor's Quarterly Stock Report.* Most public libraries subscribe to at least one of these references.

Here are a few tips on the fastest and most painless calculation of net quick assets per share from the information in the stock guides. Remember that net quick assets are short-term assets minus short-term liabilities minus long-term liabilities. To get past the accounting jargon which obscures the financial information shown in the stock guide, you need two additional facts. First, short-term assets minus short-term liabilities is listed as *working capital.* Second, long-term liabilities are listed as *senior capital*. So all that is necessary is to subtract the figure for senior capital from working capital. This difference will be the net quick assets, and division by the number of outstanding shares yields the net quick assets per share. If the senior capital is larger than the working capital, then net quick assets are negative, and one simply moves on to the next company listed in the stock guide.

PRINCIPLES OF SELLING

Why does one stock decline only 20 percent in a major bear market, while a second stock declines 50 percent, a third stock 70 percent, and a fourth stock 90 percent in the same market? There are almost as many reasons for these different rates of decline as there are stocks. The task ahead is to arrive at general selection principles for predicting declining prices—principles that will apply more or less equally to all stocks.

The practical question, then, is: Can we predict these different rates of decline before the bear market begins? The answer is a qualified yes. We can predict these declines with an accuracy that lies somewhere between pure chance and perfect stock selection. In other words, the principles of selling will enable us to beat the market averages on our sales or short sales, but there is no guarantee that any single stock sold is going to decline more steeply than the averages. The valuation of individual stocks always presents an element of risk, and the risk is probably greater than the risk in market forecasting. An adequate market forecasting system will be right about 80 percent or 85 percent of the time, while a decent system of stock selection will beat the market averages only 70 percent to 75 percent of the time.

Selling Principle 1: The Price/Earnings Ratio

The price/earnings ratio for any stock is its current selling price divided by its earnings per share for the last 12 months. If a stock currently sells for $50 and its earnings for the last year are $5 per share, then its P/E ratio is 10 ($50 ÷ $5 = 10). A stock selling for $60 with annual earnings of $12 per share has a P/E ratio of 5 ($60 ÷ $12 = 5), and a stock selling for $33 with recent earnings of $1.50 per share has a P/E ratio of 22 ($33 ÷ $1.50 = 22). Every stock has a P/E ratio except for issues of companies which have no earnings or net operating losses for the last 12 months.

The P/E ratio is our predictor of how much a stock will decline in a bear market. All else being equal, a stock with a P/E ratio of 40 will lose a greater percentage of its price in the bear market than a stock with a P/E ratio of, say, 8. The reason for this is that the bear market takes its greatest toll on the individual stocks that appear to be most overvalued, and stocks selling for 30 or 50 times their annual earnings will look absurdly overvalued compared to issues selling for five or six times their earnings. Inevitably, stocks in the first category will be driven down 60 percent to 80 percent in the bear market, whereas the stocks at lower P/E ratios will decline only 30 percent to 50 percent in the same market. Here is the first principle of selling:

> *For bear market forecasts,* SELL *(or sell short) the stocks with the highest price/earnings ratios.*

Now let's demonstrate this principle for real stock price data in bear markets and see exactly how much profit can be made by shorting the stocks with the highest P/E ratios. Our research sample again consists of the 100 stocks shown in Table 1 at the bull market top of January 1973.

Abbott Laboratories sold for $40 per share in January 1973, with 1972 earnings of $1.44 per share, and its P/E ratio at that time was 28. ACF Industries sold for 48 with earnings of $3.40 and a P/E ratio of 13, Acme-Cleveland sold for 17 with earnings of $.83 and a P/E ratio of 21, and so forth. There is a P/E ratio for every issue in our 100-stock sample except American Bakeries, the only corporation listed in Table 1 that lost money in 1972.

Now the 100 stocks in our sample declined an average of 53 percent in the 1973–1974 bear market. If instead of shorting all 100 stocks in Table 1 we had shorted only those stocks with the highest P/E ratios, the profitability of our short-selling would have been increased. Table 30 shows the results of shorting the 15 stocks with the highest P/E ratios (36 or higher) in January 1973. These 15 stocks declined an average of 68 percent versus an average decline of 53 percent for all 100 stocks.

A second way of testing the validity of the P/E ratio as a predictor of stock declines in bear markets would be to compare the declines of the stocks with the lowest P/E ratios to the average decline. Sixteen of the 100 stocks shown in Table 1 had P/E ratios of 10 or lower in January 1973. If Selling Principle 1 is valid, then these 16 stocks should have

TABLE 30
Bear market declines for 15 stocks with highest price/earnings ratios.

Stock	P/E Ratios	Bull Market High, January 1973	Bear Market Low, October 1974	Percent Decline
Alexander's	(36)	9	2	77%
Amerada Hess	(40)	48	12	75
American Air Filter	(39)	40	5	87
American Airlines	(120)	25	4	84
American Bakeries	(nil)	11	3	72
American Building Maintenance	(39)	47	4	91
American Home Products	(39)	124	78	37
American Hospital Supply	(52)	52	12	65
AMP	(48)	126	61	52
Automatic Data Processing	(82)	94	20	79
Avery International	(47)	43	22	49
Avon Products	(64)	138	18	87
Baxter Laboratories	(80)	61	24	61
Beckman Instruments	(66)	45	17	62
Black & Decker	(56)	117	61	48
Average Decline: 68%				

declined less than average in the 1973–1974 bear market. In fact, these 16 stocks with the lowest P/E ratios declined an average of 41 percent in the bear market, while the average stock in Table 1 declined 53 percent.

Future Prospects for Selling Principle 1

In bear markets, stocks with the highest P/E ratios have consistently declined more than the market averages. Conversely, stocks with the lowest P/E ratios have consistently declined less than the averages in the same bear markets. The full-time market player will want to validate Selling Principle 1 with real price data from additional samples and other bear markets, but my overall impression is that issues with the highest P/E ratios have consistently declined 15 percent to 20 percent more than the average during major bear markets, while issues with lowest P/E ratios have declined 10 percent to 15 percent less than the averages.

It is likely that Selling Principle 1 will remain profitable in future market cycles. Stocks which have been bid up to 40, 50, and even 60 times their annual earnings are issues whose prices reflect unusual investor optimism about future corporate earnings. There can be no doubt that different companies have different prospects and that some corporations grow more rapidly than others, but the rosiest corporate future has already been discounted in the price of a stock selling for 50 or 60 times earnings. The next bear market is almost certain to arrive before all of the anticipated profits are realized. The bear market begins, general business conditions begin to deteriorate a few months later, and eventually the confidence of investors is shaken. Given the poor business climate and rapidly falling expectations, these same high P/E stocks that were beneficiaries of optimism during the bull market are now special victims of investor pessimism during the bear market. Stocks with the highest P/E ratios come to look absurdly overpriced, and these are the issues that decline most in the bear market. This process will probably continue in future market cycles.

Another contingency of Selling Principle 1 that the alert market player should keep in mind is that the exact values of the highest P/E ratios may be different at each bull market top. This is not important in itself. What is important is to sell (or sell short) the stocks with the highest P/E ratios relative to the rest of the market. At the January 1973 market top, for example, stocks selling for 40 and 50 times annual earnings were common, and stocks selling for 60 and 70 times earnings were not exactly scarce. The highest P/E ratios were somewhat lower at the market tops of January 1966, December 1968, and January 1977. In particular, so many investors and institutions took a bath in the 1973–1974 bear market that there was more concern with the relationship of price to earnings in the most recent bull market than in previous markets. This caution kept P/E ratios at the January 1977 market top well below the excessive values that were reached in January 1973. Nevertheless, the highest P/E ratios are always defined relative to the P/E ratios of the entire market before the bear swing begins.

For Selling Principle 1 the additional loss following an unexpected market advance is negligible. The player who sells or shorts stocks with high P/E ratios and then finds the market averages advancing, say, 7 percent, will also lose about 7 percent on his sales. In general, he will lose no more or less on his sales than the percentage the market average moves against his position. The probable results of an incorrect market forecast differ for each selling principle, and we will deal with this problem for each principle of individual stock sale.

Recency and Availability of Data for Selling Principle 1

P/E ratios are printed in newspaper listings of stock. *The Wall Street Journal* or the financial section of any metropolitan newspaper lists each stock, its dividend rate, and its P/E ratio before the sales volume and price action for the previous day. The listed P/E ratio is the current selling price of the stock divided by the last 12 months of earnings. Most corporations report earnings on a quarterly basis, and the most recent figures are usually available two to four weeks after the end of the latest fiscal quarter. The most recent quarterly earnings are then averaged into the P/E ratio as soon as they are reported.

Selling Principle 2: The Dividend Yield

The second characteristic of stocks that determines how much each issue will decline in a major bear market is the dividend yield. The dividend yield for any stock is calculated as a percentage of that stock's selling price. For example, a stock that sells for $100 with a dividend of $3 per year has a dividend yield of 3 percent ($3 ÷ $100). A stock that sells for $40 with a $2 annual dividend yields 5 percent ($2 ÷ 40), and a stock that sells for $25 with a $1.75 annual dividend has a yield of 7 percent ($1.75 ÷ $25). The dividend yield is our second predictor of how much different stocks will decline in a major bear market. In general, stocks with higher dividend yields will not decline as much as stocks with lower dividend yields. The most important reason for this relationship is that a higher dividend yield tends to support the selling price of its stock and thus limits the extent of its decline. Two brief examples will make the point clear.

First, consider a stock selling for $100 with a yearly dividend of $6, or a 6 percent yield. If the stock drops to 90, the $6 dividend now yields 6.7 percent. With the stock at 80 and the same dividend, the yield rises to 7.5 percent. If the stock drops to 50, the $6 dividend would provide a 12 percent yield. But chances are excellent that the stock will never drop as low as 50, because the $6 dividend will enable the stock to attract buyers at 70 or 65. Only a complete market crash combined with an extremely severe credit squeeze could drive the stock much below $50, as long as the $6 annual dividend is paid on schedule.

Now consider a second stock selling for $100 with a yearly dividend of $1, or a yield of 1 percent. This stock receives virtually no support from its dividend in a major bear market. If the stock drops to 50, the $1 dividend holds the yield to 2 percent. A 2 percent yield will not in itself attract much interest in the stock. The stock can drop to 25, and the yield will increase to only 4 percent. The stock will have to drop below 17 before the yield even reaches 6 percent.

When the 11 predictors of the S&P 500 forecast a bear market ahead, the player should sell (or sell short) those stocks with the lowest dividend yields. These stocks will have consistently declined more than the market averages by the time the bear market bottoms out. Here, then, is Selling Principle 2:

> *For bear market forecasts,* SELL *(or sell short) the stocks with the lowest dividend yields.*

Let's demonstrate and validate Selling Principle 2 for real stock price data in the 1973–1974 bear market. Of the 100 stocks shown in Table 1, 21 issues had dividend yields of less than 1 percent at the January 1973 market top. How much did these low-yield stocks decline in the bear market of 1973–1974? Table 31 shows that these 21 stocks declined an average of 65 percent versus an average decline of 53 percent for the entire list of 100 stocks. You should also note that 15 of the 21 stocks declined more than the average of 53 percent, while six stocks declined less than the 53 percent average. In summary, Selling Principle 2 was correct in 15 of its 21 selections, or about 71 percent of the time.

If Selling Principle 2 is valid, then the reverse should apply to the stocks with the highest dividend yields at the January 1973 market top. These high-yield stocks should have declined less than the 53 percent average in the 1973–1974 bear market. Nine of the 100 stocks in Table 1 yielded dividends of 6 percent or more in January 1973, and these nine issues declined an average of 38 percent, while the average stock dropped 53 percent of its price in the 1973–1974 bear market.

TABLE 31
Bear market declines for 21 stocks with dividend yields below 1 percent.

Stock	Bull Market High January 1973	Bear Market Low October 1974	Percent Decline
Air Products & Chemicals	75	68	10
Alpha Portland Industries	17	6	64
Amerada Hess	48	12	75
American Airlines	25	4	84
American Building Maintenance	47	4	91
American District Telegraph	61	15	76
American Hospital Supply	52	18	65
American Motors	8	3	62
AMP	126	61	52
Anaconda	29	16	44
ARA Services	155	47	70
Automatic Data Processing	94	20	79
Avery International	43	22	49
Avon Products	138	18	87
Bache Group	10	2	80
Baxter Laboratories	61	24	61
Bearings	59	21	64
Beckman Instruments	45	17	62
Becton, Dickinson	44	21	52
Berkey Photo	22	1	95
Black & Decker	117	61	48
Average Decline: 65%			

Future Prospects for Selling Principle 2

I think Selling Principle 2 will continue to identify stocks that will decline more than the market averages in bear markets. If the professional market player tests this principle for additional samples of stocks in other bear markets, he will find that stocks with the lowest dividend yields consistently decline 10 percent to 15 percent more than the market averages, and that stocks with the highest yields consistently decline 20 percent to 30 percent less than the average. The reasoning that underlies Selling Principle 2 is so basic to the operation of security markets that it would require a complete transformation of present investment practices to distort the selecting power of the principle. Sufficiently high dividend yields will support the price of virtually any stock during an adverse market swing, and they will continue to do so in future bear markets. It would take a very unlikely chain of events to distort this principle. However, since the alert market player should be aware of the most hypothetical possibilities, try to imagine the following scenario. Amid an absolutely catastrophic bear market (worse than 1929–1933), short-term interest rates soar to, say 18 percent, and corporate earnings plunge to virtually nothing. Dividends are cut, and the market averages decline 90 percent or 95 percent. There is no money to purchase stock at any price in the ensuing depression. Under such extreme circumstances the dividend yield at the last bull market top might lose its power to select the stocks that declined most or least. Barring such unlikely events, it is unlikely that the selecting power of Selling Principle 2 will be distorted in future bear markets.

Finally, we must deal with the problem of applying Selling Principle 2 when the bear market forecast is incorrect, as it will probably be about 10 percent or 15 percent of the time. The player who has sold or shorted stocks with low dividend yields and then finds the market advancing against his position will probably lose slightly more than the percentage of the adverse market move. How much more? My research suggests about 15 percent more. For example, if the market averages advance 10 percent against the player who has shorted low-yield stocks, his losses will probably be about 11.5 percent. Since there is a tendency for stocks with lowest dividend yield to be slightly more volatile than average, these stocks will outpace the rising market averages if the bear forecast is wrong. In sum, an incorrect market forecast with Selling Principle 2 will be more costly than an incorrect forecast with Selling Principle 1. Accordingly, the player should be more certain of his bear market forecast before using the second selling principle.

Recency and Availability of Data for Selling Principle 2

The dividend payout for each stock is listed in the stock tables of *The Wall Street Journal* and your local newspaper. The amount of the annual dividend is printed between the name of the stock and the P/E ratio. To obtain the dividend yield, divide the closing price of the stock by the dividend. When a company changes the amount of its dividend, the new dividend is listed in the stock tables immediately after the change is announced. Cuts in dividends have been fairly infrequent during recent bear markets, and they have invariably followed large declines in corporate earnings. In other words, the bad news is already out and reflected in the price of the stock before the reduced dividend is announced. By this time the bear market has already been falling for several months, and I doubt if the player will beat the market averages by shorting stocks with reduced dividends.

Selling Principle 3: Previous Bull Market Advance

Selling Principle 3 is the opposite of Buying Principle 1. There is no question that different stocks should advance at different rates in bull markets. Different corporations have different earnings and vastly different prospects, and it is reasonable to expect one stock to double in a bull market that averages a 50 percent advance while a second stock advances only 20 percent or 30 percent in the same market. However, every bull market will have several stocks which triple and quadruple and a few which increase five, six, or seven times in price. No matter how favorable a company's prospects, speculative enthusiasm has been overdone when that company's stock is driven to a five- or sixfold increase in a single bull market. When the bear market finally gets under way, this optimism turns to pessimism, and it is these biggest winners of the last bull market that now look most ridiculously overpriced in the light of more pessimistic investment opinion. Accordingly, it is the same stocks that performed best in the last bull market that now perform worst in the bear market. In fact, the bear market is likely to overdo its devaluation of these stocks, and these issues may be seriously undervalued by the time the market bottoms out (Buying Principle 1). The circumstances of overvaluation at the bull market top and undervaluation at the bear market bottom make for large percentage declines in those stocks during the market declines.

This leads to Selling Principle 3:

> *For bear market forecasts,* SELL (*or sell short*) *the stocks that have advanced most in the previous bull market.*

How well does Selling Principle 3 work for our research sample of 100 stocks (Table 1)? To test the principle, I calculated the advance of each stock in Table 1 from the previous bear market bottom of July 1970 to the bull market top of January 1973. Two of the stocks were not listed in July 1970, and the bull market advances for the remaining 98 stocks were quite variable. Of these 98 issues, 14 stocks at least tripled in price during the 1971–1972 bull market. What happened to these stocks, which had gained 200 percent or more, when the bull market topped out in January 1973? Table 32 provides the answer. These 14 stocks declined an average of 70 percent while the average decline for all 100 stocks was 53 percent. Eleven of the 14 stocks declined more than 53 percent, giving Selling Principle 3 a selection accuracy of 79 percent for this sample.

If Selling Principle 3 is sound, the stocks with the smallest advances in the 1971–1972 bull market should have also suffered the smallest decline in the 1973–1974 bear market. There were ten stocks that gained 15 percent or less in price in the 1971–72 bull market. These ten stocks declined an average of only 33 percent in the 1973–1974 bear market, considerably less than the 53 average decline for all 100 stocks in the same market.

Let's summarize the results of Selling Principle 3. Starting from a total of 100 stocks with an average 53 percent de-

TABLE 32
Bear market declines for 14 stocks that tripled in the previous bull market.

Stocks	Bull Market High January 1973	Bear Market Low October 1974	Percent Decline
American Broadcasting	80	22	72
American Building Maintenance	47	4	91
American District Telegraph	61	15	76
American Sterilizer	40	11	72
AMF	57	9	84
AMP	126	61	52
Arvin Industries	26	4	85
Automatic Data Processing	94	20	79
Baker International	71	45	37
Baxter Laboratories	61	24	61
Bearings	59	21	64
Beech Aircraft	24	10	58
Berkey Photo	22	1	95
Black & Decker	117	61	48
Average Decline: 70%			

cline, the principle selected 14 issues that declined an average of 70 percent in the bear market. Reversal of the principle then selected ten stocks that declined only 33 percent instead of 53 percent. The accuracy of the principle for individual stock selection is greater than either of the first two selling principles. However, the risks of using Selling Principle 3 are also greater.

Future Prospects for Selling Principle 3

Individual stocks will continue to differ in volatility during future market cycles, and high volatility will probably remain a two-way street for the market player. Stocks which have risen three, four, and five times in value during any bull market will decline more steeply than the averages in the bear market that follows. However, this relationship is quite general, and the market player would not be well advised to develop specific indexes of volatility for individual stocks.

Several Wall Street professionals have already experimented with specific volatility indexes for different stocks, and the use of beta values (or coefficients of volatility) became quite fashionable in the market research of the early 1970s. These beta values did not enable the average fund manager (who can't forecast the market either) to beat the market averages, and they have since gone the way of most Wall Street fads.

It is tempting but not really profitable to calculate volatility coefficients for individual stocks, and here's the reason why. If a market player compiles one list of 10 or 15 stocks that have risen 200 percent and a second list of stocks that have risen only 20 percent in the same bull market, he can be reasonably certain that the average stock on the first list will decline more than the average stock on the second list in the subsequent bear market. But the player cannot be certain that the average stock which increased, say, 400 percent will do worse in the next bear market than the average stock which increased only 250 percent. Similarly, the average stock that increased 80 percent may not do noticeably worse in the bear market than the stock that increased only 60 percent. In other words, Selling Principle 3 is far too general to be used for small and medium differences in volatility, and the market player should not try to impose false precision on what is a very general selling principle. It is enough to be certain that the biggest winners in the last bull market will be larger-than-average losers in the next bear market.

The human psychology that underlies Selling Principle 3 provides additional assurance that this selection principle will continue to function in future bear markets. In bull markets with average 40 percent or 50 percent increases, stocks with four- and fivefold price increases are invariably objects of much outright speculation. The initial price increases in these stocks lead to considerable publicity. Sales volume increases, and a very active market develops for these stocks. The brokerage firms, which seldom advise caution in bull markets (or at any other time), start to hustle these early winners to their individual and institutional clients. Thus, a stock which doubled in the first swing of a new bull market may double again as the "street" gets its sales and publicity campaigns into gear. If the stock is in reasonably short supply, the company's prospects are reasonably good, and the bull market is reasonably long, the stock may actually double a third time. But the party is over when the bull market tops out. These same stocks which have been bid up to five and six times their original price can easily lose 80 percent, 85 percent, and even 90 percent of that price in a bear market that loses only 35 percent or 40 percent on the average issue. In fact, the disenchantment of investors with these big winners of the last bull market is probably as overdone as the speculative enthusiasm that originally drove up the price. By the time the bear market ends, many of the biggest losers will now be seriously undervalued (Buying Principle 1).

The player will beat the bear market averages if he sells (or sells short) the biggest winners of the last bull market, but he will probably do even better if he combines Selling Principle 3 with some additional selection principles for bear markets. Here there is no need to be especially concerned with P/E ratios and dividend yields. (The P/E ratios will be extraordinarily high and the dividend yields abysmally low for all the biggest winners by the end of the bull market.) However, application of Selling Principle 3 to companies which have only recently been listed, whose stock is selling well, and which are showing declining earnings before the bull market top would probably yield average short-sale profits of 80 percent instead of 70 percent.

Just as Selling Principle 3 yields greater bear market profits than the first two selling principles, it will also yield the greatest loss if the player's market forecast is wrong. These are exceptionally volatile stocks, and if the market averages advance against one's short position, the losses will be greater than the simple percentage gain of the averages. For example, if the market averages advance 10 percent against the player, his loss on the issues selected by this principle will probably average 13 percent or 14 percent. Accurate forecasting is more essential to the profitability of this selling principle than of the first two principles.

Recency and Availability of Data for Selling Principle 3

Recency presents no problem for this principle. If a bull market has been advancing strongly and the 11 forecasting indicators suddenly predict a bear market ahead, here's what to do. Compare the current selling price of each stock with its selling price at the bottom of the last bear market. The stocks which tripled or more between the last bear market bottom and today are the stocks which are also going to decline more than average in the next bear market.

Since the last bear market will probably have ended two, three, or several years ago, you will need stock charts to determine each selling price at the last bear market bottom. *Moody's Handbook of Common Stocks* charts 1,000 stocks, and the *Value Line Investment Survey* charts 1,700 stocks. Both concentrate on issues which trade on the New York Stock Exchange plus a few major stocks traded on the secondary exchanges. Charts for stocks which are not covered by *Moody's* and the *Value Line* will be found in *Standard & Poor's Stock Reports*, a quarterly publication that charts virtually all stocks. Do *not* obtain the prices for previous bear market lows from a back issue of *The Wall Street Journal, Barron's,* your local newspaper, or any other nongraphic source. These will cause your calculations to miss the stock splits and stock dividends that have been declared since the end of the last bear market. *Standard & Poor's Stock Reports* are available at all large libraries, most medium-size libraries, and many smaller libraries. The *Value Line* publications are even more widely distributed, and just about every library has a copy of *Moody's.*

4/Indicators That Don't Work

THE following market indicators have been quite popular on Wall Street during the last two decades. This information alone should give the alert market player plenty of reason for suspicion, because professional money managers have consistently underperformed the stock market averages. In this chapter I will discuss ten of the indicators that have helped the fund managers lose your money, and nearly everyone else's money, from 1965 to 1978. If you steer clear of these indicators, you may leave something for your children.

There are several reasons why the alert market player should be as familiar with the market indicators which have failed as with the indicators which have worked. First, historical knowledge of indicators that have failed provides some protection against being victimized by minor variations of the same indicators in the future. Wall Street and much of the financial press have short memories. Knowledge of indicators which have failed is one of the alert market player's best protections against the extravagant claims of financial writers and stockbrokers who present old indicators in new clothing. Second, market conditions will always vary from cycle to cycle. Understanding why some of the most successful indicators of 25 years ago are worthless today is an important step toward understanding why some of today's best indicators may be equally useless 25 years hence. Finally, virtually all indicators follow from ideas about the specific conditions that advance and depress stock market prices. In a very real sense, then, the failure of a forecasting indicator is the failure of a specific idea. In a manner similar to Gresham's law, bad ideas seem to drive out good ideas, and the history of professional money management indicates that Wall Street is never short of bad ideas for playing the market. The alert market player who is determined to trade by his own ideas will profit from dissecting the bad ideas of others. Here are ten ideas which have cost market traders millions of dollars.

ODD LOTS

The odd-lot indicator is based on the simple idea of two distinct groups of market traders: a group of large traders, who always win, and a group of small speculators, who invariably lose. Since the small trader is presumed to lack the capital to buy and sell individual stocks in round lots (that is, numbers of shares in units of even hundreds), he must necessarily trade in odd lots.

The basic idea is that the large trader consistently skins the small trader, so the player who uses an odd-lot indicator simply does the opposite of the small trader. In other words, the market player buys when the volume of odd-lot selling exceeds the volume of odd-lot buying, but he sells when odd-lot purchases run ahead of sales. Thus, instead of getting skinned, the market player supposedly gets in on the skinning.

It is possible that the odd-lot indicator forecasted earlier market cycles, but it has not done so between 1965 and 1977, the period under study. My analyses of odd-lot transactions and the market averages show virtually no relationship between the two series for the past 13 years. Furthermore, the basic idea which underlies the odd-lot indicator is probably not applicable to the markets of the last two decades. For example, odd-lot transactions presently account for less than 5 percent of average daily market volume. It is most unlikely that the remaining 95 percent of market players are enriching themselves from pickings as slim as these. Finally, there is some indirect evidence that odd-lotters actually outperformed the S&P 500 through the complete market cycle of 1970 through 1974. Institutions were heavy buyers of exceptionally volatile issues in the last years of the 1972 bull market, and many institutions sold these same stocks for huge losses toward the end of the 1973–1974 bear market.

The greatest problem with any "smart money vs. dumb money" approach to market forecasting is to identify those individuals and groups (if any) which sold to the institutions at the bull market top and repurchased their shares at the market bottom only two years later. Identification of these individuals would be difficult, but it would be far more profitable than trying to forecast the market with odd-lot transactions. On-balance odd-lot action appears to predict nothing.

CONFIDENCE INDEX

This is another casualty of the "smart vs. dumb money" approach to market forecasting. In comparison with odd lots, the specific idea that underlies the Confidence Index is fairly complicated. Indeed, many of the professional money managers who have lost millions by following the Confidence Index cannot explain how the indicator is supposed to work. This being the case, there is absolutely no reason for expecting these same managers to understand why the Confidence Index has failed to work through the market cycles of 1965 to 1978.

The Confidence Index is a ratio of the average yields on high-grade corporate bonds to the average yield on low-grade corporate bonds. According to the theory of confidence, the flow of money between high- and low-grade bonds is an indicator of future market averages. Why? The two scenarios run something like this. When a bear market is imminent, the "smart" money evades risk by moving from low-grade bonds to high-grade bonds. This increases the yield of the low-grade bonds while it depresses the yields of the higher-grade bonds, so the Confidence Index declines. Following the same line of reasoning, the opposite sequence unfolds just before a major bull market gets under way. The "smart" money shifts from higher- to lower-grade corporate bonds, the yields increase for the former but decline for the latter, and the Confidence Index advances.

Now that you understand how the Confidence Index is supposed to forecast the market averages, the most important fact you should know is that the Index failed to forecast the market averages between 1965 and 1977. Possibly the Index worked prior to 1965, but it hasn't worked recently. The largest problem with the Confidence Index is the false distinction between the "smart" money, which allegedly knows which way the market will move, and the "dumb" money, which doesn't. There is little evidence that any identifiable group (corporate insiders, security analysts, brokers, speculators, institutions, and so on) consistently outperforms competing groups in the market. This is not to deny that certain individuals may consistently outperform other individuals in forecasting the market, but the winners and losers probably cannot be distinguished by their memberships in different groups.

A second problem with the theory of confidence is that if the so-called "smart" money could really forecast the major market swings, it would certainly trade stocks instead of bonds. For those who can forecast the market averages, there is simply no reason to play around with bonds. The exception, of course, might be certain institutional investors which are legally obligated to keep a fixed percentage of their assets in bonds. But the evidence suggests that institutional market forecasting has led to losses rather than profits.

In summary, the Confidence Index has failed to forecast the market averages from 1965 through 1977, and it's highly questionable if the indicator worked before 1965. Moreover, the basic theory of confidence is probably inadequate to explain the major market swings of the last two decades. In general, all market indicators based on distinctions between "smart" money and "dumb" money should be regarded with special skepticism by the alert market player.

SHORT INTEREST

The short-interest ratio is another popular market indicator that has received sporadic attention from the sorcerers of Wall Street. The indicator is the ratio of the total short positions for a specific month to average daily market volume for the same month. Several financial writers have contended that increasing short-interest ratios precede major market advances while decreasing short-interest ratios forecast major declines. These same authorities hardly ever present evidence in support of their belief. The clearest explanation that has been proposed for this market indicator is that short interest measures latent demand for stocks, because the bears must eventually buy into the market in order to cover their short positions.

In my own study of the relationship between monthly short interest and the S&P 500 for 1965–1977, I found some evidence for higher short-interest ratios at bear market bottoms and lower ratios at bull market tops. However, this relationship was quite weak, and I was unable to construct any profitable trading rules for playing the market with the short-interest ratio. Another discouraging feature of the short-interest ratio also appeared in my analysis. Specifically, the market averages appear to run well ahead of the short-interest ratio, rather than vice versa.

To understand the failure of the short-interest ratio as a market indicator, the alert market player might consider several of the following possibilities. First, the fundamental idea that short interest represents a future demand for stock may not be accurate. Many short sales represent hedges by traders who are "locking in" profits from long positions that must be held for tax purposes. Additional short sales arise from arbitrage operations of individual traders, brokerage firms, and other financial institutions. Short sales of hedgers and arbitragers are eventually covered by delivery of shares on hand rather than by purchasers in the open market. A second problem with this market indicator is that the absolute number of short sales is fairly constant through a complete cycle, while average daily sales volume is always much greater at bull market tops than at bear market bottoms. In other words, a high short-interest ratio might decline as volume increases on the first bull market swing, but this would not provide evidence that short covering contributes to the advance. Finally, there is some evidence that short positions are usually too small and the market too liquid for reliable predictions of the S&P 500 from short-interest indicators. Indeed, one major study of short sellers in the 1960s showed that the average speculative short position is held for about two weeks whereas the average long position is held for about two years. Thus, it is unlikely that complete biweekly turnovers of short positions could have much impact on intermediate- and long-term market swings.

To summarize our discussion of the short-interest ratio as a market forecasting indicator: the indicator has not worked from 1965 to 1978, and it is not clear that it worked for previous market cycles either. The short-interest ratio also appears to lag rather than lead the market averages. Finally, much of the reasoning which supports the use of this indicator is probably not applicable to recent market cycles.

SECONDARY DISTRIBUTIONS

When the larger shareholders of major corporations want to sell, a secondary distribution is frequently arranged in order to support the price of the stock that is being sold. The secondary percentage is simply the ratio of secondary sales to total stock volume for a specific market period. Numerous financial writers have proposed that the monthly changes in the secondary percentage can be interpreted as profitable indicators of future market movements.

In this particular variation of the "smart vs. dumb money" approach, an increasing secondary percentage is seen as evidence that the large shareholders want out because the market averages will soon decline. Conversely, when the principal corporate owners are holding their stock, the secondary percentage declines and the S&P 500 is supposed to advance. Does the secondary percentage actually forecast major and intermediate market swings? The answer to this question is that the indicator worked for the market cycles between 1960 and 1967 but failed to work from 1968 through 1977. An indicator so inconsistent must be regarded with considerable suspicion for future forecasting purposes. Of course, it is always possible that the secondary percentage will recover its forecasting power in future market cycles. But for now the alert market player should take a "wait and see" attitude toward the secondary percentage.

Beyond the fact that the secondary percentage has failed to forecast the market swings of the last decade, there may also be serious problems with the basic idea. First, large owners and other corporate insiders may sell for many reasons other than an immediate market decline. Need for cash, settlements of estates, and tax payments are just a few of the more likely possibilities. Second, it should be recalled that large owners buy as well as sell stocks, but the secondary percentage only reflects selling. If the corporate owners and other insiders are geniuses at forecasting the S&P 500 (which I very much doubt), the alert market player would probably do better to design an indicator based on monthly purchase/sales ratios of corporate insiders. Finally, there is a clear trend of increasing legal restriction on the stock transactions of all corporate insiders. For example, insiders who buy and sell stock on the basis of information not available to the public are now liable to legal prosecution. Similarly, in the late 1960s the courts invalidated sales of stocks by certain brokerage firms which were given advance notice of declining earnings for the Penn Central Railroad and Lockheed Aircraft corporations.

To summarize our discussion of the secondary percentage: the indicator showed some forecasting value through the early and middle 1960s, but it has not forecast the market averages for the last ten years. The rationale for the indicator is probably less applicable to present market cycles than to previous cycles, and, in any case, there are increasing legal restraints on the transactions of corporate insiders. However, an indicator which has forecasted previous market cycles and then failed for more recent cycles is usually worth watching, and the alert market player should probably take this kind of attitude toward the secondary percentage.

TOTAL CORPORATE EARNINGS

There is no question that a market player who can accurately predict the future earnings of specific corporations can buy stocks that consistently outperform the S&P 500. But a number of careful studies have shown that it is extraordinarily difficult to predict changing earnings of individual companies for as short a period as a single year. Although the changing earnings of individual companies are basically unpredictable, total corporate earnings can be forecast with reasonable accuracy on a year-to-year basis. This possibility, in turn, has led several money managers and financial writers to believe that total corporate earnings are accurate predictors of future market swings.

In order to test the forecasting power of the total-earnings indicator, I compared annual stock price data and market averages for the last 47 years. In 24 years total corporate earnings and the market averages moved in the same direction (that is, either advanced or declined together). But in 23 of the last 47 years stock prices and total earnings moved in opposite directions. In other words, this evidence suggests that even if the market player accurately forecasts corporate earnings for the next 12 months, he has no better than a 50/50 chance of correctly forecasting the market for the same period.

Closer analysis of these data clarifies the problems that arise from trying to forecast the market from corporate earnings. There is a relationship between the two series, but it is actually a case of market changes leading earnings changes, rather than vice versa. The lead time is usually from 12 to 15 months, and this explains why earnings and market changes tend to coincide in the late stages of the major market swings. In sum, an indicator which does no better than 50/50 on the market averages and which lags the market by over a year is not likely to develop into a profitable market forecaster.

LEADING STOCKS AND INDUSTRIES

One of the favorite notions of the Wall Street crowd and the financial press is the fantasy that price changes appear in specific stocks (and industrial groups) before the same changes occur in the entire market. In the past decades several issues have been proposed for this distinction as "bellwether" stocks, and it is invariably one of the more heavily capitalized blue chips that is supposed to lead the major market swings. From the 1930s through the 1950s, for example, General Motors, U.S. Steel, and AT&T were frequently touted as issues which lead the market. The same market leadership was attributed to IBM and Sperry Rand in the 1960s, and several oil service and pharmaceutical stocks have been cast in the leadership role through the 1970s.

The idea of forecasting the entire market from a single issue sounds too good to be true, and the evidence suggests that it is too good to be true. Detailed studies of several complete market cycles from the 1950s to the 1970s have shown that no single stock or industrial grouping consistently leads the market averages. There is a clear tendency for the separate stocks in various industrial groups to participate in the same price movements during the same time period, but this finding has no forecasting value in itself.

Another popular idea that is closely related to the notion of leading stocks is the belief that the market averages can be forecast by following the price action of so-called "counter-cyclical" stocks. These are issues which are believed to reveal the direction of future market swings by moving opposite to the present market averages. Sears, Roebuck and Woolworth have frequently been touted as leading examples of counter-cyclical issues, but the evidence in support of this idea is even worse than the evidence for leading stocks or industrial groups. Since most stocks move with the intermediate market swings and virtually all stocks move with the major market swings, the idea of counter-cyclical issues is suspect in any case. The exception to this rule might be shares in gold mining and gold processing corporations, and the alert market player should check to see if gold stocks are true counter-cyclicals. If they are, it would then be advisable to directly compare the market forecasting power of gold stocks with the forecasting power of gold prices (Predictor 9). Apart from gold shares, I doubt if the ideas of leading stocks and counter-cyclical stocks are promising enough to warrant further research.

MARKET P/E RATIOS

In Chapter 3 we saw that inflated price/earnings ratios at bull market tops are useful for predicting declines in bear markets. Moreover, the best bargains at the end of major bear markets usually sell for extraordinarily low price/earnings ratios. These two facts have led some authorities of Wall Street and the financial press to assume that the entire market (as well as individual stocks) fluctuates around a hypothetical or "true" price/earnings ratio. Accordingly, the unwary market player is frequently advised to buy when the price/earnings ratio for the entire market is below this true value and to sell (or sell short) when the market P/E ratio is above the same value.

The most serious forecasting problem with the idea of a true market P/E ratio is the decision about a specific buy/sell value for the market P/E ratio. For example, should the S&P 500 sell for five times earnings, ten times earnings, or fifty times earnings? The last 50 years of stock prices offer no specific ratio that tells the market player when the P/E ratio for the S&P 500 is too high or too low. A second problem is that data for the last 110 years show complete market cycles averaging about four to five years. Thus, a low P/E ratio can decline much farther before a major bear market bottoms out, and a comparatively high P/E ratio may continue to advance for several months (and sometimes years) before the end of a major bull market. In summary, the general idea of a true P/E ratio for the entire S&P 500 does reflect an understanding of the cyclical character of stock market prices. However, this understanding does not provide market forecasting power in its own right, because it is impossible to specify a value below which stock prices consistently advance and above which stock prices consistently decline. There is no question that stock prices fluctuate between high and low P/E ratios. But it is also the case that bull markets (and bear markets) continue until they reverse. Since neither generalization can specify the exact point at which a particular market swing will top out or bottom out, neither provides the forecasting accuracy that is most important to the winning market player.

TOTAL STOCK VOLUME

It is another observation of long standing that more shares of stock change hands at bull market tops than at bear market bottoms. This finding has led numerous financial authorities to the mistaken belief that careful study of total volume is useful for predicting the market averages. Indeed, there are so many different approaches to trading the market with volume that it is impossible to describe (much less evaluate) all the possibilities. The most basic idea, of course, is that increasing volume forecasts higher stock prices, while declining volume forecasts lower prices. My data for 1965 through 1977 not only suggest that this basic volume indicator doesn't work, but they also indicate that market price changes lead changes in volume, rather than vice versa.

Since there is clearly no simple relationship between total volume and future market prices, a number of authorities have suggested that market changes might be forecast by more complex definitions of volume. For example, volume can be divided among advancing and declining issues. Another approach is to study the market forecasting potential of volume in the context of the most active stocks during a specific time period. For example, it is frequently contended that market declines on high volume with activity in the blue chips are bearish, while identical declines on high volume with activity in cheaper stocks are bullish. There are several additional combinations that result from the consideration of daily (weekly, monthly) volume in the context of price and leadership, and each combination is purported to have specific forecasting implications for future market swings.

On the basis of stock price data from 1965 through 1977, it appears that neither the most basic nor the more complex volume indicators have actually forecast the S&P 500. Since the market consistently leads volume rather than vice versa, it is unlikely that the most complicated approaches to volume will yield accurate market forecasting. Finally, the alert market player should bear in mind that volume has probably been the most important variable studied by market technicians who attempt to forecast future price changes with stock charts. The complete failure of charting methods to forecast the direction of future price action is most impres-

sive evidence that volume does not help the trader to forecast the market averages.

MONEY SUPPLIES

Various measures of the nation's total money supply have
provided one of the most recent philosophers' stones of
market forecasting. According to the economists who write
the weekly market letters for the major brokerage firms,
monetary theory can be used to forecast future market
changes. The basic idea of monetary theory is that increased
money supplies cause stock prices to advance, whereas decreased money supplies cause declining stock prices.

Not only is a monetary approach to stock prices open to
serious question in its own right, but the principal measure
of the money supply, M_1, has failed to forecast stock prices
since 1959. Indeed, the S&P 500 has consistently led M_1 by
several months, rather than M_1 leading the market, and the
more inclusive measures of the money supply, M_2 and M_3,
lag several additional months behind M_1. It is not likely that
measures which lag the market by as much time as M_1, M_2,
and M_3 can be developed into useful forecasting indicators.

Any useful monetary theory of stock price forecasting
must recognize that all investments compete with many
other pressing demands on the money in circulation. Moreover, equities are only one of several media that compete
among themselves for the investment dollar. Neither of
these limitations is recognized by those who attempt to forecast the market exclusively on the basis of money supplies.
The alert market player who wants to experiment with monetary approaches to market forecasting should first develop
a measure of the money that is available for purposes of investment and speculation. It might then be possible to estimate the proportion of investment and speculative money
that is likely to be channeled into equities in the next few
months. Finally, specific market forecasts might be con-

structed from monthly or quarterly changes in this second figure. In any case, the principal measures of the nation's total money supply have probably been too general to permit accurate market forecasting in the last 18 years, and there is no reason to believe that this problem will be overcome in future market cycles.

NEW OFFERINGS

Our final popular indicator that has failed to predict the market averages is the frequency of new stock offerings. Since new offerings always occur more frequently at bull market tops than at bear market bottoms, forecasters who follow supply-and-demand theories of stock prices typically urge the market trader to buy when new offerings increase and sell when new offerings decline.

My own data from the most recent 13 years of stock prices and new offerings clearly show that the market averages lead new offerings by seven to ten months. Thus, new offerings probably lag too far behind most market cycles to provide profitable forecasting. As with many of the other measures that fail to forecast the market averages, new offerings run so far behind the major market swings that it may not be worth the effort to study any indicator that is based exclusively on theories of supply and demand.

Apart from a small band of highly reactionary economists, there has been increasing recognition of the possibility that constraints of supply and demand simply do not determine prices in speculative markets. This is especially true of speculative markets in which the items of trade (for example, equities) are neither perishable nor consumed. In the case of common stocks, an increase in price will sometimes bring out more sellers, thus stabilizing price. But the same price increase can just as easily lead potential sellers to hold their shares with the expectation of even higher prices later. Similarly, price declines lead to equally unpredictable consequences in speculative markets. Traders may stabilize prices with purchases following the decline, but they may also delay their purchases because they expect even lower prices in the future. These expectations of higher or lower prices comprise the basic psychology of all speculative markets, and at many times this psychology is a more important determinant of price changes than are supply and demand.

While it is unlikely that new offerings will provide profitable forecasting of future market cycles, none of these criticisms should be interpreted to mean that other types of supply/demand analyses are useless for the selection of individual stocks. As indicated in Chapter 3, considerations such as outstanding shares vs. floating supply, typical volume, liquidity, and specific types of ownership can help the trader select specific issues that will outperform the market averages. Certain combinations of these variables might also enable the market player to predict the S&P 500, but new offerings have virtually no forecasting power by themselves.

Appendix

Historical Data on Eleven Market Predictors

Stock Market Prices 1965–1977
The Standard & Poor 500

1965		1968		1971	
Jan.	86.12	Jan.	95.04	Jan.	93.49
Feb.	86.75	Feb.	90.75	Feb.	97.11
March	86.83	March	89.09	March	99.60
April	87.97	April	95.67	April	103.04
May	87.28	May	97.87	May	101.64
June	85.04	June	100.53	June	99.72
July	84.91	July	100.30	July	99.00
Aug.	86.49	Aug.	98.11	Aug.	97.24
Sept.	89.38	Sept.	101.34	Sept.	99.40
Oct.	91.39	Oct.	103.76	Oct.	97.29
Nov.	92.39	Nov.	105.40	Nov.	92.78
Dec.	91.73	Dec.	106.48	Dec.	99.17
1966		**1969**		**1972**	
Jan.	93.32	Jan.	102.04	Jan.	103.30
Feb.	92.69	Feb.	101.46	Feb.	105.24
March	88.88	March	99.30	March	107.67
April	91.60	April	101.26	April	108.81
May	86.78	May	104.62	May	107.65
June	86.06	June	99.14	June	108.01
July	85.84	July	94.71	July	107.21
Aug.	80.65	Aug.	94.18	Aug.	111.01
Sept.	77.81	Sept.	94.51	Sept.	109.37
Oct.	77.13	Oct.	95.56	Oct.	109.56
Nov.	80.99	Nov.	96.21	Nov.	115.05
Dec.	81.33	Dec.	91.11	Dec.	117.50
1967		**1970**		**1973**	
Jan.	84.45	Jan.	90.31	Jan.	118.42
Feb.	87.36	Feb.	87.16	Feb.	114.62
March	89.42	March	88.65	March	112.42
April	90.96	April	85.95	April	110.27
May	92.59	May	76.06	May	107.22
June	91.43	June	75.59	June	104.75
July	93.01	July	75.72	July	105.83
Aug.	94.49	Aug.	77.92	Aug.	103.80
Sept.	95.81	Sept.	82.58	Sept.	105.61
Oct.	95.66	Oct.	84.37	Oct.	109.84
Nov.	92.66	Nov.	84.28	Nov.	102.03
Dec.	95.30	Dec.	90.05	Dec.	94.78

1974		1976	
Jan.	96.11	Jan.	96.86
Feb.	93.45	Feb.	100.64
March	97.44	March	101.08
April	92.46	April	101.93
May	89.67	May	101.16
June	89.79	June	101.77
July	82.82	July	104.20
Aug.	76.03	Aug.	103.29
Sept.	68.12	Sept.	105.45
Oct.	69.44	Oct.	101.89
Nov.	71.74	Nov.	101.19
Dec.	67.07	Dec.	106.50
1975		1977	
Jan.	72.56	Jan.	102.81
Feb.	80.10	Feb.	100.96
March	83.78	March	100.57
April	84.72	April	99.05
May	90.10	May	98.76
June	92.49	June	99.23
July	92.49	July	100.18
Aug.	85.71	Aug.	97.75
Sept.	84.67	Sept.	96.23
Oct.	88.57	Oct.	93.74
Nov.	90.07	Nov.	94.28
Dec.	88.70	Dec.	91.00

Interest Rates 1965–1977
Three-Month Treasury Bills

1965		1968		1971	
Jan.	3.82	Jan.	5.08	Jan.	4.49
Feb.	3.93	Feb.	5.00	Feb.	3.77
March	3.94	March	5.14	March	3.32
April	3.93	April	5.37	April	3.78
May	3.89	May	5.62	May	4.14
June	3.81	June	5.54	June	4.70
July	3.83	July	5.38	July	5.04
Aug.	3.83	Aug.	5.09	Aug.	5.08
Sept.	3.91	Sept.	5.20	Sept.	4.67
Oct.	4.03	Oct.	5.33	Oct.	4.49
Nov.	4.08	Nov.	5.50	Nov.	4.19
Dec.	4.36	Dec.	5.92	Dec.	4.02
1966		**1969**		**1972**	
Jan.	4.60	Jan.	6.18	Jan.	3.40
Feb.	4.67	Feb.	6.16	Feb.	3.18
March	4.62	March	6.08	March	3.72
April	4.61	April	6.15	April	3.72
May	4.64	May	6.08	May	3.65
June	4.54	June	6.50	June	3.87
July	4.86	July	7.00	July	4.06
Aug.	4.93	Aug.	7.01	Aug.	4.01
Sept.	5.36	Sept.	7.13	Sept.	4.65
Oct.	5.38	Oct.	7.04	Oct.	4.72
Nov.	5.34	Nov.	7.19	Nov.	4.77
Dec.	5.01	Dec.	7.72	Dec.	5.06
1967		**1970**		**1973**	
Jan.	4.76	Jan.	7.91	Jan.	5.31
Feb.	4.55	Feb.	7.16	Feb.	5.56
March	4.29	March	6.71	March	6.05
April	3.85	April	6.48	April	6.29
May	3.64	May	7.04	May	6.35
June	3.48	June	6.74	June	7.18
July	4.31	July	6.47	July	8.02
Aug.	4.28	Aug.	6.41	Aug.	8.67
Sept.	4.45	Sept.	6.24	Sept.	8.48
Oct.	4.59	Oct.	5.93	Oct.	7.16
Nov.	4.77	Nov.	5.29	Nov.	7.87
Dec.	5.01	Dec.	4.86	Dec.	7.36

1974		1976	
Jan.	7.76	Jan.	4.96
Feb.	7.06	Feb.	4.85
March	7.99	March	5.05
April	8.23	April	4.88
May	8.43	May	5.19
June	8.15	June	5.44
July	7.75	July	5.28
Aug.	8.74	Aug.	5.15
Sept.	8.36	Sept.	5.08
Oct.	7.24	Oct.	4.93
Nov.	7.59	Nov.	4.81
Dec.	7.18	Dec.	4.35
1975		**1977**	
Jan.	6.49	Jan.	4.61
Feb.	5.58	Feb.	4.54
March	5.54	March	4.94
April	5.69	April	5.04
May	5.32	May	5.15
June	5.19	June	5.50
July	6.16	July	5.77
Aug.	6.46	Aug.	6.19
Sept.	6.38	Sept.	6.16
Oct.	6.08	Oct.	6.24
Nov.	5.47	Nov.	6.50
Dec.	5.50	Dec.	6.60

Savings Deposits 1965–1977
Total Time Deposits
(in millions of dollars)

1965		1968		1971	
Jan.	69,234	Jan.	104,178	Jan.	123,072
Feb.	70,341	Feb.	104,961	Feb.	125,800
March	71,140	March	104,696	March	129,128
April	72,081	April	104,080	April	129,293
May	72,996	May	104,171	May	131,110
June	73,818	June	104,105	June	131,856
July	74,760	July	106,411	July	132,932
Aug.	75,896	Aug.	108,259	Aug.	134,161
Sept.	76,276	Sept.	109,359	Sept.	136,161
Oct.	77,170	Oct.	110,771	Oct.	137,160
Nov.	77,662	Nov.	111,937	Nov.	138,217
Dec.	78,260	Dec.	112,163	Dec.	140,932
1966		**1969**		**1972**	
Jan.	78,868	Jan.	110,032	Jan.	142,532
Feb.	79,600	Feb.	109,213	Feb.	144,286
March	81,001	March	108,389	March	144,863
April	81,813	April	106,949	April	147,113
May	82,695	May	106,188	May	149,081
June	90,185	June	103,138	June	149,647
July	91,018	July	100,601	July	152,111
Aug.	91,255	Aug.	98,580	Aug.	155,495
Sept.	90,379	Sept.	97,977	Sept.	156,270
Oct.	88,735	Oct.	97,170	Oct.	157,686
Nov.	88,383	Nov.	96,167	Nov.	158,858
Dec.	89,639	Dec.	96,589	Dec.	160,661
1967		**1970**		**1973**	
Jan.	92,985	Jan.	95,017	Jan.	162,936
Feb.	94,240	Feb.	95,621	Feb.	168,312
March	96,133	March	98,229	March	174,299
April	96,569	April	99,281	April	176,383
May	97,829	May	99,536	May	180,341
June	98,847	June	101,580	June	179,960
July	100,731	July	106,495	July	185,434
Aug.	101,827	Aug.	110,633	Aug.	190,776
Sept.	101,659	Sept.	113,635	Sept.	189,784
Oct.	102,189	Oct.	114,820	Oct.	188,702
Nov.	102,969	Nov.	116,426	Nov.	186,481
Dec.	102,921	Dec.	119,443	Dec.	189,643

1974		1976	
Jan.	193,136	Jan.	225,352
Feb.	192,829	Feb.	223,215
March	197,888	March	225,981
April	203,689	April	221,601
May	209,557	May	222,692
June	211,529	June	225,469
July	216,232	July	223,252
Aug.	219,453	Aug.	221,423
Sept.	221,496	Sept.	223,690
Oct.	219,890	Oct.	221,646
Nov.	218,965	Nov.	224,828
Dec.	228,045	Dec.	231,416
1975		1977	
Jan.	226,719	Jan.	230,446
Feb.	224,440	Feb.	230,598
March	226,136	March	234,857
April	223,520	April	231,856
May	225,929	May	235,803
June	223,211	June	237,934
July	222,475	July	238,498
Aug.	222,765	Aug.	239,513
Sept.	225,264	Sept.	241,749
Oct.	224,960	Oct.	243,106
Nov.	225,877	Nov.	246,729
Dec.	227,729	Dec.	252,424

Authorized Housing Permits 1965–1977
One-Family Structures
(in thousands)

1965		1968		1971	
Jan.	734	Jan.	685	Jan.	816
Feb.	713	Feb.	720	Feb.	774
March	711	March	687	March	830
April	677	April	672	April	865
May	722	May	667	May	932
June	703	June	655	June	929
July	704	July	688	July	978
Aug.	692	Aug.	700	Aug.	922
Sept.	677	Sept.	732	Sept.	900
Oct.	741	Oct.	714	Oct.	920
Nov.	736	Nov.	731	Nov.	965
Dec.	745	Dec.	709	Dec.	982
1966		**1969**		**1972**	
Jan.	711	Jan.	687	Jan.	1,115
Feb.	652	Feb.	679	Feb.	992
March	743	March	660	March	1,000
April	660	April	656	April	1,008
May	596	May	639	May	961
June	574	June	644	June	1,018
July	543	July	594	July	1,027
Aug.	491	Aug.	591	Aug.	1,074
Sept.	450	Sept.	583	Sept.	1,050
Oct.	434	Oct.	582	Oct.	1,150
Nov.	441	Nov.	590	Nov.	1,033
Dec.	492	Dec.	607	Dec.	1,034
1967		**1970**		**1973**	
Jan.	582	Jan.	482	Jan.	1,108
Feb.	573	Feb.	556	Feb.	1,074
March	566	March	542	March	992
April	604	April	594	April	938
May	634	May	600	May	957
June	670	June	619	June	932
July	675	July	638	July	897
Aug.	693	Aug.	576	Aug.	825
Sept.	694	Sept.	679	Sept.	812
Oct.	697	Oct.	697	Oct.	689
Nov.	658	Nov.	703	Nov.	691
Dec.	715	Dec.	876	Dec.	665

1974		1976	
Jan.	660	Jan.	854
Feb.	715	Feb.	858
March	747	March	866
April	719	April	819
May	685	May	817
June	674	June	834
July	638	July	866
Aug.	626	Aug.	876
Sept.	588	Sept.	914
Oct.	550	Oct.	987
Nov.	534	Nov.	1,056
Dec.	514	Dec.	1,047
1975		1977	
Jan.	527	Jan.	930
Feb.	528	Feb.	1,060
March	532	March	1,188
April	616	April	1,051
May	657	May	1,077
June	671	June	1,105
July	697	July	1,089
Aug.	726	Aug.	1,156
Sept.	763	Sept.	1,135
Oct.	786	Oct.	1,216
Nov.	805	Nov.	1,257
Dec.	810	Dec.	1,126

Brokers' Cash Accounts 1965–1977
Customers' Credit Balances
(in millions of dollars)

1965		1968		1971	
Jan.	1,207	Jan.	2,942	Jan.	2,080
Feb.	1,254	Feb.	2,778	Feb.	2,259
March	1,264	March	2,692	March	2,333
April	1,207	April	2,979	April	2,216
May	1,208	May	3,064	May	2,084
June	1,297	June	3,293	June	2,023
July	1,233	July	3,269	July	1,841
Aug.	1,192	Aug.	2,984	Aug.	1,838
Sept.	1,369	Sept.	3,126	Sept.	1,734
Oct.	1,475	Oct.	3,407	Oct.	1,765
Nov.	1,479	Nov.	3,419	Nov.	1,758
Dec.	1,666	Dec.	3,717	Dec.	1,837
1966		**1969**		**1972**	
Jan.	1,730	Jan.	3,597	Jan.	2,040
Feb.	1,765	Feb.	3,647	Feb.	2,108
March	1,822	March	3,294	March	2,070
April	1,744	April	3,077	April	2,030
May	1,839	May	3,084	May	1,930
June	1,658	June	3,084	June	1,845
July	1,595	July	2,783	July	1,842
Aug.	1,595	Aug.	2,577	Aug.	1,733
Sept.	1,528	Sept.	2,579	Sept.	1,677
Oct.	1,520	Oct.	2,753	Oct.	1,708
Nov.	1,532	Nov.	2,613	Nov.	1,828
Dec.	1,769	Dec.	2,803	Dec.	1,957
1967		**1970**		**1973**	
Jan.	1,914	Jan.	2,626	Jan.	1,833
Feb.	1,936	Feb.	2,463	Feb.	1,770
March	2,135	March	2,441	March	1,719
April	2,078	April	2,248	April	1,536
May	2,220	May	2,222	May	1,564
June	2,231	June	2,009	June	1,472
July	2,341	July	2,180	July	1,542
Aug.	2,281	Aug.	2,083	Aug.	1,462
Sept.	2,401	Sept.	2,236	Sept.	1,632
Oct.	2,513	Oct.	2,163	Oct.	1,713
Nov.	2,500	Nov.	2,197	Nov.	1,685
Dec.	2,763	Dec.	2,286	Dec.	1,700

1974		1976	
Jan.	1,666	Jan.	1,975
Feb.	1,604	Feb.	2,065
March	1,583	March	1,935
April	1,440	April	1,740
May	1,420	May	1,655
June	1,360	June	1,680
July	1,391	July	1,635
Aug.	1,382	Aug.	1,605
Sept.	1,354	Sept.	1,710
Oct.	1,419	Oct.	1,580
Nov.	1,447	Nov.	1,740
Dec.	1,424	Dec.	1,855
1975		1977	
Jan.	1,450	Jan.	1,930
Feb.	1,610	Feb.	1,815
March	1,770	March	1,720
April	1,790	April	1,715
May	1,705	May	1,710
June	1,790	June	1,805
July	1,710	July	1,860
Aug.	1,500	Aug.	1,745
Sept.	1,455	Sept.	1,745
Oct.	1,495	Oct.	1,850
Nov.	1,470	Nov.	1,845
Dec.	1,525	Dec.	2,060

Call Loan Interest Rate 1965–1977
New York Stock Exchange

1965		1968		1971	
Jan.	4.50	Jan.	5.08	Jan.	6.28
Feb.	4.50	Feb.	4.97	Feb.	5.88
March	4.50	March	5.14	March	5.49
April	4.55	April	5.37	April	5.32
May	4.75	May	5.62	May	5.50
June	4.75	June	5.54	June	5.50
July	4.75	July	5.38	July	5.93
Aug.	4.75	Aug.	5.09	Aug.	6.00
Sept.	4.75	Sept.	5.20	Sept.	6.00
Oct.	4.75	Oct.	5.33	Oct.	5.92
Nov.	4.75	Nov.	5.50	Nov.	5.53
Dec.	4.97	Dec.	5.91	Dec.	5.36
1966		**1969**		**1972**	
Jan.	5.07	Jan.	6.18	Jan.	4.89
Feb.	5.25	Feb.	6.16	Feb.	4.63
March	5.41	March	6.08	March	4.55
April	5.50	April	6.15	April	4.88
May	5.50	May	6.08	May	5.00
June	5.52	June	6.50	June	5.00
July	6.00	July	7.00	July	5.23
Aug.	6.12	Aug.	7.01	Aug.	5.25
Sept.	6.25	Sept.	7.13	Sept.	5.25
Oct.	6.25	Oct.	7.04	Oct.	5.70
Nov.	6.25	Nov.	7.19	Nov.	5.75
Dec.	6.25	Dec.	7.72	Dec.	5.75
1967		**1970**		**1973**	
Jan.	4.76	Jan.	7.91	Jan.	6.01
Feb.	4.55	Feb.	7.16	Feb.	6.29
March	4.29	March	6.71	March	6.80
April	3.85	April	6.48	April	7.00
May	3.64	May	7.04	May	7.18
June	3.48	June	6.74	June	7.83
July	4.31	July	6.47	July	8.41
Aug.	4.28	Aug.	6.41	Aug.	9.41
Sept.	4.45	Sept.	6.24	Sept.	10.04
Oct.	4.59	Oct.	5.92	Oct.	10.02
Nov.	4.76	Nov.	5.29	Nov.	10.00
Dec.	5.01	Dec.	4.86	Dec.	10.00

1974		1976	
Jan.	9.95	Jan.	7.55
Feb.	9.39	Feb.	7.40
March	9.08	March	7.38
April	10.23	April	7.38
May	11.48	May	6.88
June	11.78	June	7.31
July	12.22	July	7.50
Aug.	12.25	Aug.	7.50
Sept.	12.25	Sept.	7.50
Oct.	11.80	Oct.	7.50
Nov.	10.81	Nov.	7.50
Dec.	10.50	Dec.	7.50
1975		**1977**	
Jan.	10.11	Jan.	7.50
Feb.	9.02	Feb.	7.50
March	8.09	March	7.50
April	7.66	April	7.50
May	7.42	May	8.00
June	7.15	June	8.00
July	7.30	July	8.25
Aug.	7.84	Aug.	8.50
Sept.	8.06	Sept.	8.25
Oct.	8.22	Oct.	9.25
Nov.	7.76	Nov.	9.25
Dec.	7.64	Dec.	9.00

Real Wages 1965–1977
Spendable Weekly Earnings per Employed Worker
(in constant dollars)

1965		1968		1971	
Jan.	87.17	Jan.	90.16	Jan.	91.68
Feb.	87.28	Feb.	90.92	Feb.	92.06
March	87.41	March	90.76	March	92.14
April	87.34	April	90.11	April	92.54
May	87.67	May	91.30	May	92.35
June	88.02	June	91.88	June	92.39
July	87.94	July	91.93	July	92.15
Aug.	88.13	Aug.	92.16	Aug.	92.62
Sept.	88.07	Sept.	92.85	Sept.	92.56
Oct.	87.79	Oct.	91.91	Oct.	93.32
Nov.	88.45	Nov.	91.00	Nov.	93.57
Dec.	88.57	Dec.	91.64	Dec.	93.89
1966		**1969**		**1972**	
Jan.	87.42	Jan.	90.67	Jan.	95.72
Feb.	87.59	Feb.	90.17	Feb.	95.80
March	87.63	March	90.31	March	96.24
April	88.17	April	90.26	April	96.94
May	87.47	May	91.00	May	96.19
June	87.89	June	91.31	June	96.49
July	88.43	July	91.37	July	96.76
Aug.	88.30	Aug.	91.44	Aug.	97.10
Sept.	87.13	Sept.	92.17	Sept.	97.19
Oct.	88.48	Oct.	91.20	Oct.	97.79
Nov.	88.12	Nov.	90.53	Nov.	97.72
Dec.	89.46	Dec.	90.61	Dec.	97.63
1967		**1970**		**1973**	
Jan.	90.53	Jan.	90.00	Jan.	96.42
Feb.	89.89	Feb.	89.83	Feb.	96.76
March	89.92	March	89.84	March	96.40
April	89.62	April	89.11	April	96.34
May	90.38	May	89.44	May	95.83
June	91.05	June	90.35	June	95.89
July	91.63	July	90.99	July	96.23
Aug.	91.57	Aug.	91.34	Aug.	94.78
Sept.	91.86	Sept.	90.55	Sept.	95.18
Oct.	91.16	Oct.	89.63	Oct.	94.58
Nov.	91.19	Nov.	89.35	Nov.	94.66
Dec.	90.93	Dec.	89.81	Dec.	94.22

1974		1976	
Jan.	92.94	Jan.	91.60
Feb.	92.75	Feb.	92.00
March	91.99	March	91.45
April	90.91	April	91.41
May	91.62	May	91.91
June	91.34	June	91.42
July	91.37	July	91.47
Aug.	90.68	Aug.	91.36
Sept.	90.16	Sept.	91.30
Oct.	89.91	Oct.	91.88
Nov.	88.61	Nov.	92.24
Dec.	88.67	Dec.	92.18
1975		**1977**	
Jan.	88.42	Jan.	91.36
Feb.	87.83	Feb.	91.80
March	87.64	March	91.69
April	87.53	April	91.58
May	91.76	May	91.69
June	91.60	June	94.93
July	91.27	July	95.12
Aug.	91.73	Aug.	94.73
Sept.	91.90	Sept.	95.04
Oct.	91.86	Oct.	96.16
Nov.	92.03	Nov.	95.62
Dec.	92.14	Dec.	95.66

Bankers' Security Loans 1965–1977
Purchasing or Carrying Securities
(in millions of dollars)

1965		1968		1971	
Jan.	6,368	Jan.	8,350	Jan.	7,282
Feb.	6,151	Feb.	7,562	Feb.	6,866
March	6,449	March	6,578	March	7,256
April	6,573	April	6,938	April	6,719
May	6,803	May	6,736	May	7,014
June	7,418	June	7,689	June	7,599
July	5,712	July	8,839	July	6,719
Aug.	6,224	Aug.	8,751	Aug.	7,707
Sept.	5,453	Sept.	10,245	Sept.	7,743
Oct.	5,587	Oct.	8,296	Oct.	7,787
Nov.	6,482	Nov.	7,697	Nov.	8,675
Dec.	6,420	Dec.	9,563	Dec.	8,835
1966		**1969**		**1972**	
Jan.	6,429	Jan.	7,591	Jan.	8,839
Feb.	6,249	Feb.	7,234	Feb.	9,760
March	6,035	March	7,026	March	9,520
April	6,666	April	7,233	April	10,624
May	6,784	May	6,927	May	10,477
June	6,972	June	7,564	June	10,588
July	6,139	July	7,276	July	11,423
Aug.	6,496	Aug.	7,727	Aug.	10,924
Sept.	5,821	Sept.	6,588	Sept.	11,279
Oct.	5,703	Oct.	6,261	Oct.	12,218
Nov.	5,335	Nov.	6,521	Nov.	11,868
Dec.	6,691	Dec.	7,811	Dec.	12,535
1967		**1970**		**1973**	
Jan.	7,419	Jan.	5,960	Jan.	12,007
Feb.	6,799	Feb.	6,246	Feb.	11,457
March	6,642	March	7,191	March	10,672
April	6,901	April	6,493	April	10,054
May	6,302	May	6,089	May	10,120
June	6,050	June	5,934	June	9,700
July	7,454	July	5,934	July	12,128
Aug.	7,024	Aug.	6,235	Aug.	9,640
Sept.	7,247	Sept.	6,091	Sept.	9,301
Oct.	7,791	Oct.	6,436	Oct.	9,508
Nov.	6,817	Nov.	7,153	Nov.	9,182
Dec.	8,340	Dec.	8,560	Dec.	9,433

1974		1976	
Jan.	8,095	Jan.	6,200
Feb.	9,154	Feb.	7,389
March	8,193	March	8,468
April	8,417	April	8,679
May	7,927	May	10,024
June	4,818	June	9,875
July	9,212	July	9,443
Aug.	8,788	Aug.	11,060
Sept.	7,335	Sept.	10,109
Oct.	7,408	Oct.	11,319
Nov.	7,415	Nov.	12,617
Dec.	7,713	Dec.	12,327
1975		1977	
Jan.	6,819	Jan.	12,213
Feb.	6,097	Feb.	11,625
March	6,816	March	11,682
April	5,597	April	11,966
May	6,350	May	12,748
June	7,326	June	12,296
July	6,842	July	13,667
Aug.	6,530	Aug.	12,854
Sept.	7,040	Sept.	13,075
Oct.	6,605	Oct.	12,905
Nov.	8,206	Nov.	13,167
Dec.	8,933	Dec.	13,638

Brokers' Margin Credit 1965–1977
Customers' Debit Balances
(in millions of dollars)

1965		1968		1971	
Jan.	5,019	Jan.	7,797	Jan.	4,224
Feb.	5,038	Feb.	7,419	Feb.	4,311
March	5,085	March	7,248	March	4,531
April	5,096	April	7,701	April	4,776
May	5,154	May	8,268	May	4,874
June	5,139	June	8,728	June	4,976
July	5,887	July	8,861	July	5,050
Aug.	4,908	Aug.	8,489	Aug.	5,121
Sept.	5,016	Sept.	8,723	Sept.	5,208
Oct.	5,096	Oct.	8,859	Oct.	5,238
Nov.	5,232	Nov.	9,029	Nov.	5,198
Dec.	5,543	Dec.	9,790	Dec.	5,700
1966		**1969**		**1972**	
Jan.	5,576	Jan.	9,042	Jan.	5,989
Feb.	5,777	Feb.	9,148	Feb.	6,477
March	5,671	March	8,318	March	6,896
April	5,862	April	8,044	April	7,283
May	5,797	May	8,474	May	7,478
June	5,798	June	8,214	June	7,792
July	5,700	July	7,515	July	7,945
Aug.	5,645	Aug.	7,019	Aug.	8,060
Sept.	5,400	Sept.	7,039	Sept.	8,083
Oct.	5,216	Oct.	7,243	Oct.	8,081
Nov.	5,275	Nov.	7,111	Nov.	8,166
Dec.	5,387	Dec.	7,445	Dec.	8,180
1967		**1970**		**1973**	
Jan.	5,375	Jan.	6,683	Jan.	7,975
Feb.	5,445	Feb.	6,562	Feb.	7,773
March	5,803	March	6,353	March	7,468
April	5,896	April	5,985	April	7,293
May	5,966	May	5,433	May	6,784
June	6,195	June	5,281	June	6,416
July	6,636	July	4,807	July	6,243
Aug.	6,677	Aug.	4,206	Aug.	6,056
Sept.	6,944	Sept.	4,107	Sept.	5,949
Oct.	7,111	Oct.	4,189	Oct.	5,912
Nov.	7,200	Nov.	4,200	Nov.	5,671
Dec.	7,948	Dec.	4,208	Dec.	5,251

1974		1976	
Jan.	5,323	Jan.	5,568
Feb.	5,423	Feb.	6,115
March	5,519	March	6,575
April	5,558	April	6,856
May	5,361	May	7,103
June	5,260	June	7,248
July	4,925	July	7,519
Aug.	4,672	Aug.	7,622
Sept.	4,173	Sept.	7,707
Oct.	4,080	Oct.	7,704
Nov.	4,103	Nov.	7,790
Dec.	3,980	Dec.	8,166
1975		**1977**	
Jan.	4,086	Jan.	8,469
Feb.	4,269	Feb.	8,679
March	4,320	March	8,891
April	4,503	April	9,078
May	4,847	May	9,267
June	5,140	June	9,432
July	5,446	July	9,667
Aug.	5,365	Aug.	9,763
Sept.	5,399	Sept.	9,793
Oct.	5,448	Oct.	9,756
Nov.	5,519	Nov.	9,859
Dec.	5,540	Dec.	9,993

Corporate Bonds and Short-Term Interest Rates
1965–1977
Aaa Bond Yields and Prime Commercial Rates

	Bond Yields	Prime Rates		Bond Yields	Prime Rates
1965			**1968**		
Jan.	4.43	4.25	Jan.	6.17	5.60
Feb.	4.41	4.27	Feb.	6.10	5.50
March	4.42	4.38	March	6.11	5.64
April	4.43	4.38	April	6.21	5.81
May	4.44	4.38	May	6.27	6.18
June	4.46	4.38	June	6.28	6.25
July	4.48	4.38	July	6.24	6.19
Aug.	4.49	4.38	Aug.	6.02	5.88
Sept.	4.52	4.38	Sept.	5.97	5.82
Oct.	4.56	4.38	Oct.	6.09	5.80
Nov.	4.60	4.38	Nov.	6.19	5.92
Dec.	4.68	4.65	Dec.	6.45	6.17
1966			**1969**		
Jan.	4.74	4.82	Jan.	6.59	6.53
Feb.	4.78	4.88	Feb.	6.66	6.62
March	4.92	5.21	March	6.85	6.82
April	4.96	5.38	April	6.89	7.04
May	4.98	5.39	May	6.79	7.35
June	5.07	5.51	June	6.98	8.23
July	5.16	5.63	July	7.08	8.65
Aug.	5.31	5.85	Aug.	6.97	8.33
Sept.	5.49	5.89	Sept.	7.14	8.48
Oct.	5.41	6.00	Oct.	7.33	8.56
Nov.	5.35	6.00	Nov.	7.35	8.46
Dec.	5.39	6.00	Dec.	7.72	8.84
1967			**1970**		
Jan.	5.20	5.73	Jan.	7.91	8.78
Feb.	5.03	5.38	Feb.	7.93	8.55
March	5.13	5.24	March	7.84	8.33
April	5.11	4.83	April	7.83	8.06
May	5.24	4.67	May	8.11	8.23
June	5.44	4.65	June	8.48	8.21
July	5.58	4.92	July	8.44	8.29
Aug.	5.62	5.00	Aug.	8.13	7.90
Sept.	5.65	5.00	Sept.	8.09	7.32
Oct.	5.82	5.07	Oct.	8.03	6.85
Nov.	6.07	5.28	Nov.	8.05	6.30
Dec.	6.19	5.56	Dec.	7.64	5.73

	Bond Yields	Prime Rates		Bond Yields	Prime Rates
1971					
Jan.	7.36	5.11	July	8.72	11.72
Feb.	7.08	4.47	Aug.	9.00	11.65
March	7.21	4.19	Sept.	9.24	11.23
April	7.25	4.57	Oct.	9.27	9.36
May	7.53	5.10	Nov.	8.89	8.81
June	7.64	5.45	Dec.	8.89	8.98
July	7.64	5.75			
Aug.	7.59	5.73	**1975**		
Sept.	7.44	5.75	Jan.	8.83	7.30
Oct.	7.39	5.54	Feb.	8.62	6.33
Nov.	7.26	4.92	March	8.67	6.06
Dec.	7.25	4.74	April	8.95	6.15
			May	8.90	5.82
1972			June	8.77	5.79
Jan.	7.19	4.08	July	8.84	6.44
Feb.	7.27	3.93	Aug.	8.95	6.70
March	7.24	4.17	Sept.	8.95	6.86
April	7.30	4.58	Oct.	8.86	6.48
May	7.30	4.51	Nov.	8.78	5.91
June	7.23	4.64	Dec.	8.79	5.97
July	7.21	4.85			
Aug.	7.19	4.82	**1976**		
Sept.	7.22	5.13	Jan.	8.60	5.27
Oct.	7.21	5.30	Feb.	8.55	5.23
Nov.	7.12	5.25	March	8.52	5.37
Dec.	7.08	5.45	April	8.40	5.23
			May	8.58	5.54
1973			June	8.62	5.94
Jan.	7.15	5.78	July	8.56	5.67
Feb.	7.22	6.22	Aug.	8.45	5.47
March	7.29	6.85	Sept.	8.38	5.45
April	7.26	7.14	Oct.	8.32	5.22
May	7.29	7.27	Nov.	8.25	5.05
June	7.37	7.99	Dec.	7.98	4.70
July	7.45	9.18			
Aug.	7.68	10.21	**1977**		
Sept.	7.63	10.23	Jan.	7.96	4.70
Oct.	7.60	8.92	Feb.	8.04	4.74
Nov.	7.67	8.94	March	8.10	4.82
Dec.	7.68	9.08	April	8.04	4.87
			May	8.05	4.87
1974			June	7.95	5.35
Jan.	7.83	8.66	July	7.94	5.49
Feb.	7.85	7.83	Aug.	7.98	5.41
March	8.01	8.42	Sept.	7.92	5.84
April	8.25	9.79	Oct.	8.04	6.17
May	8.37	10.62	Nov.	8.08	6.55
June	8.47	10.96	Dec.	8.19	6.59

Gold Prices 1972–1977

1972		1974		1976	
Jan.	61	Jan.	143	Jan.	132
Feb.	64	Feb.	159	Feb.	133
March	63	March	170	March	128
April	63	April	163	April	127
May	65	May	168	May	126
June	65	June	168	June	125
July	70	July	173	July	126
Aug.	66	Aug.	156	Aug.	120
Sept.	67	Sept.	159	Sept.	119
Oct.	61	Oct.	174	Oct.	110
Nov.	64	Nov.	192	Nov.	114
Dec.	63	Dec.	174	Dec.	134
1973		**1975**		**1977**	
Jan.	70	Jan.	179	Jan.	133
Feb.	77	Feb.	175	Feb.	137
March	83	March	173	March	147
April	88	April	170	April	148
May	102	May	168	May	149
June	114	June	164	June	151
July	107	July	165	July	152
Aug.	101	Aug.	164	Aug.	155
Sept.	102	Sept.	144	Sept.	151
Oct.	107	Oct.	143	Oct.	159
Nov.	104	Nov.	143	Nov.	163
Dec.	127	Dec.	140	Dec.	161

Quarterly Federal Deficits 1965–1977
Excess Receipts or Payments
(in billions of dollars)

1965		1970		1975	
March	+4.5	March	−4.5	March	−54.5
June	+4.4	June	−14.1	June	−99.9
Sept.	−2.5	Sept.	−15.4	Sept.	−66.0
Dec.	−0.2	Dec.	−20.5	Dec.	−69.4
1966		**1971**		**1976**	
March	+2.3	March	−18.5	March	−63.8
June	+3.8	June	−23.8	June	−53.5
Sept.	−0.5	Sept.	−23.4	Sept.	−57.3
Dec.	−3.3	Dec.	−22.2	Dec.	−55.9
1967		**1972**		**1977**	
March	−11.6	March	−13.4	March	−38.8
June	−12.5	June	−20.0	June	−40.3
Sept.	−13.0	Sept.	−10.8	Sept.	−58.9
Dec.	−12.3	Dec.	−24.9	Dec.	−60.9
1968		**1973**			
March	−9.8	March	−10.9		
June	−11.2	June	−7.4		
Sept.	−3.9	Sept.	−4.8		
Dec.	−1.1	Dec.	−4.6		
1969		**1974**			
March	+9.1	March	−5.3		
June	+11.7	June	−7.9		
Sept.	+5.1	Sept.	−8.0		
Dec.	+3.4	Dec.	−25.5		

Index